END
GAME
FIRST

END GAME FIRST

FIRST

A Leadership Strategy
for Navigating a Crisis

Vice Admiral **MIKE LEFEVER,** US Navy, Retired
and **RODERICK JONES**

LIONCREST
PUBLISHING

END GAME FIRST
A Leadership Strategy for Navigating a Crisis

ISBN   978-1-5445-2756-7 *Hardcover*
          978-1-5445-2754-3 *Paperback*
          978-1-5445-2755-0 *Ebook*
          978-1-5445-3819-8 *Audiobook*

CONTENTS

For the Soldiers, Sailors, Airmen, and Marines

For the hardworking entrepreneurs

For the people at Concentric

And for Patty

INTRODUCTION

AN ADMIRAL IN THE HIMALAYAS

A CRISIS STRIKES ON ITS OWN TIME, NOT YOURS.

Nestled in between contentious countries at the feet of the Himalayas lies the disputed region of Kashmir. On its northeast border, the region is bound by the Uygur Autonomous Region; on its east sits Tibet; to the south are the Indian states of Himachal Pradesh and Punjab; in the northwest is Afghanistan; and finally, to the west, is Pakistan—all areas of contention in their own right.

Since 1972, the Pakistani- and Indian-controlled portions have been divided by a line of control. The roughly 222,000 square kilometers comprise towering mountains, sinking valleys, and near-impassable terrain. With powerful countries each

1

claiming ownership, the residents of the region grew accustomed to shifting loyalties and control. On October 8, 2005, a different kind of shift would bring the region into chaos.

Deep beneath the cities and villages, far below the beautiful hillsides and gorgeous Himalayas, two massive tectonic plates shifted. The Eurasian and Indian plates pressed tighter and tighter together, building up a potential energy more powerful than a nuclear bomb. With nowhere to go, one plate had to give in. At 8:50 a.m. local time, roughly one hundred kilometers north of the capital city of Islamabad, the plates shifted...and the energy released.

The earthquake, measuring 7.6 magnitude on the Richter scale, struck without warning. The ground at the epicenter snapped, releasing a rippling wave of energy that literally shifted the landscape as the earth above the subducted plate rushed to find its new place in the world.

At the time, most buildings in the Kashmir region were simply made, without many of the reinforcements and safety features added to earthquake-prone Los Angeles or Tokyo. Houses crumbled under the intense vibration, collapsing into ruin as the hills they were built upon liquified and ran down toward the valleys. The quake lasted seconds...but the disaster had only just begun.

Thousands of kilometers away, sailing toward the Persian Gulf, the Commander of ESG 1 (Expeditionary Strike Group ONE) sailed aboard the USS Tarawa. The 39,000-ton amphibious assault craft led a Strike Group of six ships, one submarine, and 5,500 deployed sailors and Marines. The "Eagle of the Sea" had left San Diego months earlier but now closed in on its primary objective: the Central Command Area of Operations. As the crew ended breakfast and began preparations for passing the Iranian border, the news trickled in.

Rear Admiral Mike LeFever, a veteran of the United States Navy, was handed a small packet of information containing the news of the day. He saw the highlighted bullet: earthquake in Kashmir region, 7.6, high casualty rate expected. He made a quick note of the information, but his focus was the mission. The ESG needed to deliver Marines into Iraq to support their first ever election, for some of the Strike Group to patrol the area for signs of piracy off the eastern coast of Africa, and for others to protect the safety and security of Iraqi oil pumping and distribution.

Just days earlier, he had been completing an international training exercise called Bright Star. The exercise enabled multinational ground forces to acquaint one another with tactics and equipment to improve international military cooperation for the region, while at the same time maritime forces practiced to protect the sea lanes and secure the safety of international waters. Mike had watched some of the amphibious exercises from the nearby beach with CENTCOM Commander (Central Command) General John Abizaid. The four-star asked Mike how he thought the rest of his deployment would go.

Mike knew his team and had a lot of confidence in their abilities. He felt as prepared as ever, and he talked about possible follow-on missions in the central command region. The ESG was capable of operating near Yemen, Afghanistan, Sudan, Iraq, and even Africa to target pirate activity disrupting sea lines of communication. General Abizaid commented that the plan was sound but that Mike could still end up doing something completely unexpected.

Tarawa Expeditionary Strike Group (ESG) 1 in 2005.

As ESG 1 passed through the Strait of Hormuz, Mike watched news footage of the devastation in Kashmir. The death toll would take time to verify, but at least 70,000 were expected dead, with 3.5 million left homeless. Those watching the report felt a powerful urge: the human instinct to help out those in need. Mike was pulled from his thoughts as someone shouted his name. A call came into the ship from Mike's superior officer: Vice Admiral Dave Nichols, the Fifth Fleet Commander.

The Vice Admiral began with the usual pleasantries: How goes the mission? Are you prepared for your offload of the Marines into Iraq? How is your team? Then came the ten million-dollar question: what do you think about the earthquake? Mike shared his insight with the Vice Admiral. After the briefing, Vice Admiral Nichols told Mike to "continue en route to Kuwait and be prepared for a follow-on mission to possibly support delivering supplies through the port of Karachi."

That meant that Mike's journey to offload his Marines for missions in Iraq would continue, but he might eventually need to assist with the developing situation. In this case, Mike filed away the information for later. He would have plenty of time to think about the earthquake and relief missions after his work was complete. All that would change within hours.

The battle group shifted formation as it entered the Strait of Hormuz. This close to the Iranian border, they were likely to receive some routine harassment. It's a well understood rule that sovereign nations don't like watching strangers tramp around in their backyard. The US and Iran were, at that time, experiencing increasing escalations in tension. The usual posturing as the ESG passed the border could easily intensify if it wasn't carefully monitored.

First came the usual radio calls. "You're violating territorial waters. Leave now or you will be fired upon." Then came observer drones, ships racing up only to rapidly turn away. It was a game. For the uninitiated, it could be unbearable; a war

could erupt at any moment. For Mike, it was another day at
sea. He assured his crew that they were on course, assured his
Strike Group to remain steady on, and thought of the mission
to come. They had trained for—and expected—this type of
encounter in the Strait.

Around the time Mike settled in for another briefing, this
time regarding the Marine deployment once they reached
the shore, the Vice Admiral came back for another call. As he
walked down the corridor to take the call, Mike could smell
dinner in the galley. He heard the voices of his fellow sailors,
Marines, and trained officers.

"Mike." The Vice Admiral sounded calm. It's a common thing
for superior officers to address subordinates by their first
names as a sign of respect. "Change of plans. You're leaving
at first light with a small number of your staff to head into
Bahrain—briefing en route—to lead the US military relief
effort to Pakistan." And that was it. The mission to Iraq was
delegated to his Chief of Staff and subordinate commanders.
He had a new task, a new goal...and he had no idea what to
expect on the ground.

After a brief few hours "in the rack" and a sudden wake up, it
was time to leave. Mike met with the detachment commander
and triple-checked that they were prepared to assume control
of the mission. Then it was time to board a helicopter to
Bahrain. As the MH-60 Seahawk flew into Bahrain FIFTH
Fleet Headquarters, Mike read over a small briefing packet his
staff assembled for preparation.

Information was slim, but he could tell right away that the earthquake had been far more devastating than originally reported. The epicenter was confirmed 100 kilometers north of Islamabad, but the entire region had been affected. Infrastructure had collapsed, leading to a humanitarian crisis unlike any the region had seen in a generation.

Complicating matters, Pakistan was an ally in the Global War on Terror and under great strain with the neighboring situation in Afghanistan. The situation on the ground was entirely unknown and likely to be dangerous. Still, all Mike could think about were the people that desperately needed help. He formulated a plan based on the few scenarios he'd ever worked that even came close. The US military at the time did not have any learned guidance in leading this type of contingency.

After landing in Bahrain—and receiving briefings and equipment—came a fourteen-hour flight to Islamabad. Mike knew he had to hit the ground running. Fortunately, Mike had received a briefing from the Fifth Fleet Commander discussing resources and the available information, so he relayed as much as possible to his team. The most important mission was saving lives and alleviating the situation on the ground. Infrastructure had to be rebuilt, hospitals had to be established, and rescue operations needed to get underway. This would improve relations in the area and have long-term consequences for the region. The importance of success couldn't be understated. As they touched down, Mike had a strange thought: *I'm a naval commander 700 kilometers from the nearest large body of water.* The irony was not lost on him.

An Australian S-70 Blackhawk, atop a snow-covered peak in the Himalaya Mountains. The Australians played a significant part in the earthquake relief effort.

Mike and his team disembarked the plane only to arrive in an alien world. Rescuers from countries around the world gathered at the airport, stacking clothing and supplies in a makeshift bazaar in preparation for the long weeks ahead. Everywhere Mike looked, he saw different colors and uniforms and relief organizations and support groups. It was like a scene out of Star Wars. Within hours, Mike was in the US Embassy to meet the US Ambassador to Pakistan (the distinguished Ryan Crocker, a career diplomat) and the Country Team for his initial briefings.

Mike knew this was an overwhelming mission, and he had to get control of the situation or it would grow worse as each hour passed. He just hoped he was the right person for the job.

Balakot, Pakistan was left devastated after the earthquake. Balakot is one of the largest communities in the region and the hardest hit due to its proximity to the earthquake epicenter. In the coming months, there would be 1,771 aftershocks from the initial earthquake.

With twenty-hour days, there was little time to think. Mike received constant briefings, leaving only a few minutes to consider options and make a decision. It was an alien experience, unlike any deployment or training he'd encountered before.

Mike, his staff, and the embassy Country Team endured long days and nights, but the mission to save lives drove their efforts. There was no one else on the ground wearing his name tag, so each morning he grabbed a cup of coffee and prepared for another day. Shortly after arriving, Mike received a call from his boss General Abizaid. The General reminded Mike of his comment not long ago: that he perhaps might end up doing something completely unexpected. A few weeks later, General Abizaid and his Director of Operations General Doug Lute visited Pakistan. The CENTCOM Commander congratulated Mike on a hard few weeks. They discussed the operation thus far, and then came the most difficult question of all.

"So, Mike. What's your exit strategy?"

A TALE OF TWO COMPANIES

When you start your own company, you're in love with your own idea. You have a plan, a dream, and a million possibilities dancing around in your head. It's easy to skip your end game when you're bolstered by passion. It's also easy to get in over your head and fail before you've even begun. Starting a tech company is the definition of a crisis: it's a long time before you're profitable. Therefore, you have to know that every decision can and likely will make or break your company.

Roderick began his career with Scotland Yard's Special Branch working on counter-terrorism and then leading the protection detail of a prominent member of the British cabinet. He consulted globally on the future of security with the Pentagon and Intelligence Agencies in the United States.

As he forged his own path as an entrepreneur, he sought out a familiar niche. Concentric became Roderick's first security company, and much of this book is about how Concentric is able to survive and thrive in our age of turmoil. He also founded the cybersecurity startup Rubica Inc.—which, while not the subject of this book, forms a core part of the crisis experience as it subsequently failed.

Working in cybersecurity is important in our modern, connected times, and you can quickly see the results of your work. Giant enterprise companies delivering vast solutions dominate the cybersecurity field, and when Roderick founded Rubica, a lot of good cybersecurity solutions were already available in the business-to-business arena. However, the solutions were neither widely distributed to the public nor easy to use. Rubica was to change all this and offer these solutions to a broader consumer audience and open up a new market for advanced cybersecurity.

Roderick and his Rubica team found themselves chasing a myriad of tactical problems instead of working toward a deliberate goal. They consumed the zeitgeist on how to run a successful startup. There was capital, investors, a business plan...and then nothing. Like roughly 90 percent of startups, they failed. The money ran out, the investors left, and only equal parts excess hardware and frustration remained.

Yet mistakes breed experience. When you trip and fall down, you're still moving forward. When Mike and Roderick teamed up to lead Concentric, following a change of management, they brought a shared backlog of knowledge for managing any number of crises. That's how they found the idea of the **End Game**.

Of course, no one suspected a pandemic was just around the corner. That is where their unique crisis mindsets separated them from the pack. Since these lessons are important, perhaps it's best to hear it in their own words.

The end of a startup: Rubica offices.

WELCOME TO CRISIS LEADERSHIP

Welcome. We are Mike and Roderick, and we know how hard it can be to follow advice from some faceless narrators. That's why this book is designed to be more conversational. Imagine yourself sitting across from us at a table as we share insights, anecdotes, and practical guides to managing a crisis in a leadership position.

After living through crises of all sizes and shapes, we realized that our unique understanding could be applied by just about anyone. As we share these scenarios and anecdotes, we'll talk about ourselves in the third person (or one of us might refer to the other as such). Whether we're talking to you directly or waxing about a crisis from the past, remember that we are right beside you as you journey through these pages.

If you picked up this book, you're a leader and you're in a crisis—or know you could be at any moment. We are here as your guides to learn how to recognize a crisis, how to lead through one, and how to emerge on the other side successfully.

A crisis comes in every shape and size. It can be personal, professional, or even national. Losing your job is a crisis. A car accident is a crisis. Your company facing bankruptcy is a crisis. And a global pandemic affecting billions of lives is a crisis.

We rarely enter a crisis on our own terms. It arrives without warning, hitting us at our most vulnerable, and we are left to pick up the pieces. How do you address the damage caused? How do you rebuild? And how do you navigate the "new normal" of a postcrisis world? You won't be successful if you're always waiting to react, so how do you get ahead of the curve?

In a crisis, you have to consider your **end game first**. At some point in the future, you will be out of danger and back in the day-to-day. Where do you want to be when that happens?

The end game isn't where the crisis is leading, it's where *you* want to be at the end. What is *your* "exit" strategy?

The end game is the result of your choices and actions, and it can leave you in a better place than before. It's not easy to think about the end of a crisis when you're still living through one, but you can be more successful by keeping your strategic goal in mind.

You keep sight of your end game by recognizing where you stand in the crisis timeline. A crisis follows a predictable—if dynamic—path, and you can learn to navigate it. Every crisis, no matter the scale, runs through the same phases. Understanding each phase of a crisis lets you identify how far along you are and to plan your next strategic move.

This book is designed for those in leadership positions, but it can be used by anyone who needs to make decisions in a crisis: an EMT, a business person, a family leader. No matter what the world has thrown at you, there is a path forward, and there is an "exit strategy."

FINDING YOUR END GAME

This book **provides a guide to the anatomy of a crisis** and how it is *likely* to unfold. That way you know how to be most effective as a leader during each phase. While each crisis will absolutely be unique, you can find similarities that allow you to determine phases and make the appropriate decisions. The timelines will, of course, differ depending on the scale and severity of the crisis: a traffic accident will have a far more rapid progression than a stock market collapse.

This book **builds knowledge that leads to skill**. You are holding combined decades of hands-on experience managing crises of all sizes, from natural disasters to professional collapses to military actions. While you may never go through these *exact* scenarios, we will show you how to translate them into a variety of possibilities.

This book also **helps build mental preparedness**. A crisis affects you on every level. Whether you've been through the chaos before or it's your first time, high stress leads to mental and physical wear and tear. The most important thing to keep in mind is your health and safety. It won't mean anything if you survive one crisis only to have created another.

Knowing the end game first puts you in a better position to navigate any scenario.

WHAT YOU'LL LEARN

- How to understand the phases of a crisis and how to move between them

- Universal processes for building a team and affecting change

- Effective crisis networking through managing and mapping relationships

- How to communicate effectively with your teams, clients, and competition

- How to manage your resources so you don't leave a crisis worse off

- How to spot trends, identify momentum, and prepare for a crisis

WHY ARE YOU HOLDING THIS BOOK?

In the course of writing this, we were asked a number of times, "Why are you writing this book?" Surely there are other books out there for crisis management and leadership?

We often found that other books on crisis management focused on major disasters. There's rarely any translation to more general issues that all of us will encounter.

In the same vein, leadership books focus on generalities during times of crisis. While it's easy to say, "Be a rock, be the steady guiding hand of your team," that advice doesn't apply to the entirety of a crisis. In different phases of crises, you will need to adjust your leadership to reach your end game.

As we said before, a crisis will progress through a series of phases, and these are the same no matter the scale. Other books don't explain the necessary successful behaviors for each distinct phase. That's why, in our humble opinion, this is *the* book on how to guide yourself and your team through a calamity.

WHAT THE BOOK IS AND ISN'T

This book is a general manual for understanding the distinct phases in a crisis and what to do during them. You'll be provided with clear examples of how to recognize phases, identify transition moments, and engage the right people to build out a complete team. Along the way, we will share stories from calamities of varying scale and scope, so you can see how these principles apply.

More importantly, we want you to understand the dynamics of a crisis so you'll know what success is during each distinct phase. We'll show you the difference between luck and opportunity, between events you can plan against and storms you'll just have to weather. In the end, you'll know how you and your team can reset, regroup, recover, and rebuild.

This book is not designed to teach you about managing a crisis or to have a military mindset. While Mike comes from a naval background, the lessons he learned apply to all aspects of a crisis. The scope of this book is truly from the conjoining of Mike and Roderick's different experiences, but with lessons that echoed between.

This book also isn't a step-by-step checklist of what you need to accomplish in order to reach your end game. Your specific crisis will require you to create a unique plan, and we can't account for every possible scenario here. However, if you follow our guidelines and use your common sense, you stand a better chance of emerging ahead of the game.

LET THE CALAMITIES BEGIN

Everyone holding this book has experienced a crisis. And as humans, we often don't do a great job with them. That's why we want to provide the tools that will allow you to do better when, inevitably, the next one happens.

If you're still reading, then you're ready to go on this journey. Like any crisis, there is work ahead and sweat equity to pay. We will be the guides to lead you, and we have enough information to build a stable foundation to weather the coming storms. Our recommendation is to go in at your own pace, take notes in the margins, and don't be afraid to ask questions (though the book is notoriously unlikely to answer).

CHAPTER 1

END GAME FIRST

THE OPENING HOURS OF A CRISIS OFTENTIMES MEAN the difference between life and death. If you witness a car accident, those initial few minutes will determine the course of the victim's life. As you scale a crisis, those stakes seem to scale exponentially.

Mike landed in a country at war with nature. Anyone who has witnessed the direct aftermath of a disaster can tell you the chaos is always the same: panicked victims caked in dust and blood, eager rescuers rushing in, and a world shattered. In that opening moment, watching the crisis unfold, it feels impossible to visualize what comes next.

Citizens rushing the landing of a CH-47 bringing in food and medical supplies during the early days of relief by Task Force Griffin.

The typical scene at austere village landing zones throughout the affected areas as villagers awaited food and medical supplies being delivered.

The first two weeks of Pakistan went by in a blur. There were multiple briefings each day, as information needed to be accurate up to the minute in order for Mike to make the right decisions. Military helicopters—days ago flying in combat missions—were now performing relief operations, and hundreds of personnel had to be trained on new procedures. Hospitals were built, outgrown, and expanded in hours. Then, of course, came the follow-on effects of the disaster.

Landslide north of Muzaffarabad, Pakistan that resulted in the redirect of the Jhelum River and wiped out significant infrastructure.

An earthquake is a strange experience. We generally take for granted that the ground will remain underfoot, so any change can throw equilibrium out the window. While the phenomenon lasts only seconds, the damage is often catastrophic and enduring, with aftershocks lasting up to six months after the event. The immediate chaos is bad, but natural disasters are

more than just momentary distress. Roads are damaged, pipe-
lines and infrastructure rendered unusable. This adds a new
variable to the rescue and recovery efforts. It's not enough
to find survivors, you need a means to transport them safely
away from danger, and you need to support them until they are
self-sustainable.

When General Abizaid met with Mike, he was in the middle
of assessing resources. The initial chaos from the disaster had
abated somewhat, leaving a wounded nation struggling to heal.
As Mike prepared resources to help with the recovery, his team
grew to 1,500 people on the ground, two field hospitals from
the 212 MASH (Mobile Army Surgical Hospital) unit—and
another set up by a Marine unit from Okinawa—US helicopters from countries around the region, and tens of thousands
of support staff around the globe supporting. This Joint Task
Force and Combined Forces (Australia and NATO) unit was
pointed directly at the problem, but they would only be as
effective as their leader.

All of that pressure landed on Mike's shoulders. He was happy
to see a familiar face when General Abizaid arrived. CENT-
COM oversaw two operational theaters of war: Iraq and
Afghanistan. It was a monumental amount of responsibility,
and the four-star general had decades of experience maneuvering through any number of crises. Mike knew that any
advice offered carried years of experience. He didn't expect the
General's question:

"What's your exit strategy?"

Mike's first thought was a proper paraphrasing of Captain Lloyd Williams's iconic WWI quote: "We just got here!"

The past few weeks had been a swirl of assessing, reacting, and planning. The coalition force put out a few fires immediately with helicopters, aircraft, and strategic sealift to do the initial triage. They were planning on hospitals, construction support, and resources to distribute humanitarian relief in the most rugged terrain in the world. The goal, as Mike saw it, was saving lives and providing humanitarian relief. Of course, the overall mission was to improve relations with Pakistan, but that would be an aftereffect of properly caring for its people and supporting a country in need. Mike knew that the United States military was unmatched in its ability to respond to a crisis. He had witnessed how quickly assets and personnel could arrive on-site to affect positive change. What he hadn't thought about was what the end would look like and how to get there.

The sheer scope of resources brought to bear meant that Mike could tackle a number of secondary missions...but that wasn't the crux of this crisis. He couldn't—and shouldn't—stay in Pakistan forever. While the coalition had been invited to help, they could easily overstay their welcome. Mike also couldn't keep the military and civilian personnel that had been assigned to him for long. He relayed as much to his commander.

"General, we have done assessments, and with the support of your staff we are looking at bringing in two major field hospitals located in two different affected areas of Pakistan. We'll need more helicopters, strategic airlift and sealift, and Navy

Seabees to support immediate construction needs. Finally, we need resources to extend the reach of food distribution. We'll start working on the exit strategy next."

The CENTCOM Commander nodded knowingly. "At the end of this mission, when the roads are able to bear traffic and the people are able to feed themselves, you'll need to leave. What does that look like? **What is the goal you're working toward with every decision you make?**"

Mike realized this was prescient advice: the perfect way to plan, execute, and shape how they would exit from relief operations. He was reacting when he needed to be *acting* and *planning*. He needed every decision to lead toward a single purpose. He needed to identify his end game and work toward it.

With that in mind, he called his leaders into a meeting and prepared to explain the new mindset. They were about to change the way they managed a crisis.

WHAT DOES THE END GAME LOOK LIKE?

In the initial moment of a crisis, it's okay, natural, and productive to focus on being reactive. Often, you don't have the luxury of time and space to plan out a more deliberate movement. When disaster strikes, those first few seconds are pure chaos.

In the same vein, the opening moments of *every* crisis require immediate action. If you're in the middle of a disaster, it's very hard to step outside and think about the big picture. However, those moments will come. You will eventually arrive at a point of stability and have a chance to observe your situation so you can formulate a long-term plan. At that moment, you need to see the **end game**.

The end game isn't the final act of the crisis; the end game is where you will be after the crisis has fully passed. How are you positioned? What moves will you be taking next? Most importantly, how do you shape the outcome?

A crisis changes our world in small—and enormous—ways, but we continue to move forward. By working toward where we want to be at the end of a crisis—without ignoring the important steps that must be taken—we help achieve a more positive outcome for all.

So what is your end game? Well, that all depends on the crisis you're facing.

For Pakistan, the United States wanted to build a stronger relationship with an estranged country. The immediate goals of the recovery were saving lives and rebuilding, but Mike always kept in mind that the intent of these efforts was to create a bond between the US and Pakistan. It meant that decisions made along the way always had two metrics for success: will this action/resource going to save lives, and will it build a better relationship?

A stronger relationship with Pakistan put the United States in a better strategic position for the war in Afghanistan and the war on terror. It gained a valuable ally for sharing intelligence, coordinating airspace, and staging supplies. It cooled a historically complex and—at times—heated relationship with repercussions of escalation. The geostrategic advantage could not be overstated.

On a seemingly smaller scale, the COVID-19 crisis presented a major challenge for Concentric. We were a global enterprise that was suddenly unable to travel globally. This meant we could either button up and hope to weather some serious financial loss, or radically adapt to the new circumstances and emerge even stronger than before.

When we identified our end game—emerging stronger in terms of capabilities, clients, and diversification—we realized the opportunity that a restructure could have for our business.

With the world evolving to a remote and distributed model, our security solutions needed to adapt to emerging threats. Since we were ahead of the curve, we quickly became the go-to for a number of major clients. Suddenly, we weren't facing a financial crisis but rather a staffing crisis, in that we needed to staff up as quickly as possible.

There is risk with any decision made during a crisis, but it is always better than standing still. If you don't identify and act in accordance with the end game, you're going to be caught unaware when the world moves on without you.

When you look at a list of successful businesses, you see companies that know how to manage crises. Friend of the farmer,

John Deere, thrives because it is now a data company as much as a tractor building company. No matter your industry, from tech and design to entertainment, evolution is necessary for survival. A crisis simply accelerates that adaptation. And if you hope to not only *endure* a crisis but *thrive* in the long run, you need to have your goals aligned.

So how exactly do you keep your end game first?

CONCENTRIC IN COVID-19

Concentric is a global security company with a lot of work around the world. Part of our success depended upon access to a worldwide array of personnel and technology. We traveled extensively, connecting with clients to walk them through our security solutions. For large businesses, security is a crucial—and often sensitive—topic. Being able to sit down with a CEO and discuss solutions, or support client travel, helped us establish ourselves in a busy market.

And then international travel closed down as countries battled a pandemic.

Our initial thought immediately jumped to our families, our staff, and our clients. We had to keep our people safe and healthy. We quickly realized that the travel lockdown was going to hit us hard, to the tune of a 40 percent loss in revenue. The pandemic was evolving into a new phase, but we were entering the beginning of our own personal crisis. How could Concentric survive?

Uncertainty makes you want to draw resources in, close off. It would have been simple, even understandable, to shutter the doors and windows and hope the storm left something of value when it passed. But this wasn't our first time examining a crisis, and we knew the secret that so many forget: this too shall pass. We found our end game by realizing that *every* business now had a major pivot on their hands. Workforces were going remote, or even completely distributed. With a larger online presence came increased cybersecurity threats, so Concentric had to evolve as well.

When COVID-19 shut down international travel, it was a dire threat to our business. We were still in our growth mentality, building toward a global reach amid a saturated market. We had a goal to be recognized as the "Most Innovative, Capable, and Trusted Risk Management Partner in the World," and we couldn't reach that end game if we cut our capacity. While many companies—including our competitors—reduced over-head and laid off employees, we maintained our staff with the goal of keeping our capabilities flexible.

We pivoted the business and focused on domestic security challenges. The nature of our industry was changing rapidly: men with guns can't protect you from a virus, an online threat, or crypto-driven cyber extortion.

It was a risky decision, but one we knew we had to make. If we cut our employees and tried to wait out the crisis, who knows what the end game would have been. We might have emerged from stasis with the same business model but without the capability to meet our clients' needs. That failure would likely mean the end for Concentric. Hiring and training a new team takes time and money, both of which would be in incredibly short supply if we hid in a bunker until we could resume business as usual.

This pivot allowed us to reach out to new customers: domestic customers who were having to respond to the new environment they faced. Our staff required retraining, but that was far more sustainable than bringing in new people. When we finally connected with the right clients, the work quickly filled up. It wasn't the Concentric we had set out to build a year ago, but it was designed to survive and grow. It met our end game expectations.

Now, we have a business that is larger than our previous model, but it's completely new. That is entirely due to our willingness to pivot and keep our eye on the end game.

CHASING PROBLEMS VERSUS WORKING TOWARD A GOAL

Do you remember the story of the Hero of Haarlem? You might know it as "The Little Dutch Boy." One day, a young boy living in a small village notices that the nearby dike is leaking, threatening to flood the town. He quickly runs over and plugs the leak with his finger, waiting all night through the freezing cold until the villagers arrive to repair the damage.

It's a fine parable but a terrible lesson on crisis management. When we talk about reacting versus taking action, this is a good object lesson. You can't simply plug up one problem and wait for other people to arrive to help with the rest. The measures you take to address *each* issue have to lead somewhere. It's not enough to know your end game; you have to work toward it with every single decision.

In a crisis, every day brings new challenges. New bad news. We lost this, we don't have that, this just happened. It can quickly become overwhelming. Even if you're prepared, even if your goals are aligned, you might find yourself falling into the routine of chasing problems rather than working toward a goal.

A part of that may come from a lack of delegation. You can't do everything yourself, and trying will only exacerbate the situation. Another cause can be a lack of preparation. If you never prepared for this crisis, or even thought through the basics of *any* crisis, you can easily find yourself chasing after problems instead of staying ahead of them.

One of the most common reasons people chase problems rather than working toward a goal is simple: they are stressed. A crisis is a major test of mental fortitude, and it cannot be managed alone. We'll talk more about resilience and mental health in a future chapter, but you have to realize that these situations are going to do more than stress you out. You will be faced with decisions that have long-term consequences, and the weight of that can bear down until you feel crushed. Once you give in to that mindset, it can seem impossible to get ahead of the cascade of bad news.

This is often due to amplification. There is a lot of bad news in the early stages of a crisis, and it's amplified by everyone around you. You say it, your staff says it, your competition says it. Even seasoned professionals find it easy to fall into that spiral of negative information, until suddenly it's all you see.

The way to combat the negative spiral is to seek out—and amplify—the good. In a military environment, leaders gather together at least once a day to discuss events and update plans with the command team. At first, these sessions may require guidelines; team members might be afraid to deliver bad news to the senior leadership. A good commander will set the tone by drawing the positives out as well. When you are a leader in a crisis, it is your responsibility to hear the truth, so you can shape the situation and move forward. Advise your team to look at challenges as opportunities to take action.

Moreover, if you demonstrate every day that you are working *toward* something instead of just fighting off problems, your team sees that. Your company sees that. The mood shifts from "woe is me" to "we can do this." It's the old saying of eating the elephant one bite at a time. The tide of problems doesn't seem so strong. That feeling, knowing where things should end, can be enough to keep everyone focused on the job at hand.

BEWARE OF FEATURE CREEP

If your goals aren't clear, you may start to look for other items to add to your to-do list. Be very wary of taking on more and more work in the middle of a crisis, as it is easy to spread yourself too thin in no time at all. In the military, this is referred to as *mission creep*. In the business world, it's known as *feature creep*. Instead of completing a project and moving on, you keep adding on more and more features until it's impossible to finish.

In the primarily affected regions of Pakistan, 545,101 homes were damaged or destroyed. In one area near the epicenter, 84 percent of the homes were damaged or destroyed while in areas further away, 36 percent. Homes in this region of Pakistan were built out of either dry stacked rock and brick, or unreinforced masonry construction, making them prone to collapse with even minor seismic vibrations.

This isn't to say you can't make changes to your goals during a crisis; just remember your end game. You can't do everything, and pursuing too much can lead to a total failure.

Expansion is a risk for businesses, but one that can pay off by introducing new revenue streams. Uber expanded into food delivery. At Concentric, we expanded into webinars and online training. These were all risks, but they paid off due to hard work and careful planning.

In the middle of a crisis, these expansions can happen as well. In fact, a crisis might *demand* these sorts of risks. However, you can expand so far that you're no longer able to accomplish your goals. You can take on so much work that you're no longer effective at your primary mission. When that happens, the risk of catastrophic failure grows exponentially.

While refining your mission is necessary, allowing the scope to continually expand makes you lose focus on the end game. The way to avoid mission creep is by constantly refocusing yourself and your team on the end game. Make it a part of your daily discussions: what are you doing *today* that leads you toward your goals? If your tasks are taking you in a different direction, you've allowed the scope to veer off target.

When you lose sight of your end game, or don't have it to start with, you are failing to plan.

IF YOU FAIL TO PLAN, YOU PLAN TO FAIL

Putting the end game at the beginning of the crisis influences the decisions you make and prepares you for a successful exit.

Each choice isn't just about reacting to a new challenge. You are positioning yourself closer to your actual goals. As you continue on in this book, keep in mind the lessons from this chapter:

- The End Game is where you want to be when the crisis ends.

- While you will be reactive at the start of a crisis, you need to take charge as it moves through its phases.

- A crisis lasts for a finite amount of time. Put off certain items and tasks until after the situation has stabilized. Find your end game, create a plan, and stick to it.

FINDING THE END GAME IN PAKISTAN

After meeting with General Abizaid, Mike met with his senior leaders and discussed the new mindset. They had to think about their exit strategy. At some point in the future, the situation in Pakistan would stabilize. The homes would be rebuilt, the local forces would assume control of the hospitals and engineering efforts, and the international coalition would leave. What did that look like?

They spent hours discussing not just the logistics, but their goals for new relationships and infrastructure. They envisioned stronger ties to Pakistan that would create a stabler region overall. Once they had their end game in mind, they looked at how to build a path forward. What milestones needed to be hit in order for them to achieve these goals?

This conversation helped everyone understand not only how the crisis would end, but how everyone would shape decisions to get to that point. It created a map that anyone could follow. More importantly, it ensured that everyone was on the same page, working toward the same goal.

The leaders left the meeting confident, focused, and determined to achieve their end game.

HISTORY DOESN'T REPEAT, IT RHYMES

Concentric planned to tackle international issues, but COVID-19 shifted those plans. Roderick looked at the history of pandemics, at how businesses had evolved in 1918 when the world reacted to the Spanish flu. As it turned out, security companies pivoted then as well. A pandemic would lead to an economic shortfall, ideally eased by government intervention. That would lead to a rise in unemployment, which often correlated with a rise in property crimes. Roderick proposed that Concentric pivot away from international security consulting to more domestic issues, all while introducing a new marketing scheme.

As you move forward through a crisis, you will notice changes that seem to follow a certain scheme. We tend to imagine that each disaster is a unique event, requiring a custom solution. While the details surely differ, a crisis tends to follow a fairly predictable pattern. We refer to this as the Distinct Phases of a Disaster. A crisis begins for a number of reasons, but it progresses in common phases.

As a leader, this puts a lot of pressure on you to make the right choices at the right times. In order to be prepared to weather the storm, you need to learn how the phases ebb and flow. You need to understand the anatomy of a crisis. To paraphrase Sun Tzu, once you understand the pattern of a crisis, you need not fear any that follow.

CHAPTER 2

ANATOMY OF
A CRISIS

To understand a crisis, you need to recognize the phases of a disaster. Let's take a look at how a crisis—no matter the scale—follows a familiar pattern.

In 2010, only four years after Mike led the humanitarian effort following a devastating earthquake, a new disaster arrived in Pakistan.

Late summer in Pakistan is monsoon season, and the country is no stranger to heavy rainfall. Something was different about the growing storm cells this year though. Late July and August looked to be problematic, with a confluence of major weather events that could wreak havoc for tens of thousands of Pakistanis.

Beginning in late July, the rain fell. At first, no one suspected anything other than the normal seasonal showers. Yet, as the days turned into weeks, as the rivers overflowed, the rain persisted. Researchers in Utah noted a strange anomaly in the upper troposphere over Pakistan—a "freezing" of the jet stream, combined with an atmospheric cyclone. A monsoon of epic proportions loomed over the country, deploying a torrent of endless water.

By mid-August, 17 million acres of Pakistan were underwater, over half a million homes were destroyed, and six million people were displaced. A new crisis.

As luck would have it, Mike was already on the ground as the senior military representative.

After the earthquake (and the accomplished end game of preserved, progressed, and strong relationships), Mike became a go-to liaison with Pakistani officials. They respected the work he'd done, and his relationships opened doors for increased cooperation. In 2008, as the Iraq war entered a period of calm, Mike was assigned as the senior military representative to Pakistan as Commander, Office Defense Representative Pakistan (ODRP). He was welcomed as an old friend.

When the floodwaters rose and the nation needed support, having a leader on the ground who knew how to handle a crisis was fortuitous. At first, Pakistan only asked for a few supplies: halal MREs (combat rations, or Meals Ready to Eat) to feed refugees with culture-sensitive food items. However, they soon recognized the need for greater support.

Mobile Army Surgical Hospital (MASH) 212 in Muzaffarabad, Pakistan providing triage care to affected local Pakistani citizens. The forehead label indicates the level of triage for rapid assessment and delivery of care.

While the situation was very different from the earthquake, Mike had a sense of déjà vu. This early moment in the crisis felt almost identical. The same chaos, the same eager rescuers, the same panicked locals. It was a 911 moment, an emergency in need of immediate action. He quickly worked with the Pakistani government to establish refugee camps and water sanitation, and he began preparing for the second and third order effects. He knew from past experience how this would affect the power infrastructure, supply lines, and health care.

When the initial chaos ebbed, Mike sat down with a growing group of leaders from all around the world to plan out the humanitarian efforts in the country. Once again, he sensed a growing familiarity. This had all happened before. It wasn't just seeing the same faces, it was hearing the same terms, giving the same orders. It was history repeating, or at least rhyming. Mike decided he needed to take note of how this played out. Something important lingered just out of reach, and he intended to seize it.

As it turned out, Mike had recognized something profound: every crisis, no matter the scale or scope, follows a path. And once you know that path, you have a far greater chance of finding your end game.

THE SEQUENCE OF A CRISIS

As we mentioned in the introduction, every crisis, from a car accident to a natural disaster, follows a set of phases. Whether you're in a crisis mindset while running a startup or leading a country through a pandemic, understanding these phases is vital for your success. While you always need to keep the end game in mind, the decisions you make from phase to phase will differ drastically. You not only need to know where you are within the crisis, but how you'll transition to the next chapter or phase.

A crisis will also evolve at different rates for different parts of your organization. While Mike was moving into Phase 2 in the macro of the Pakistan flood, his aviation units were still managing Phase 1–levels of triage. It's important to recognize where the rest of your organization falls within their own scope of the crisis. These phases allow you to address the crisis in an appropriate manner, utilizing your resources to the best of your abilities.

Local villagers awaiting the arrival of food, shelter, and medical supplies. The impending onset of winter made relief operations all the more urgent.

Depending on when you are reading this book, and in which part of the world, you could be seeing an entirely different picture of the COVID-19 crisis than a reader who is in a different time or place. Your country might have fewer cases or a new variant or a new supply issue. Crises can also overlap. While you're dealing with a medical crisis, you could be impacted by a supply crisis in the Suez Canal or a new natural disaster or political turmoil.

A crisis is an overwhelming event that requires immediate action, and it evolves into an environment demanding continued maintenance and care. By the end of a crisis, you will emerge into the "normal" world, but with the knowledge of how to prevent (or mitigate) similar events in the future. So how do you recognize where a crisis begins and ends?

Any crisis, no matter the scale, has four phases:

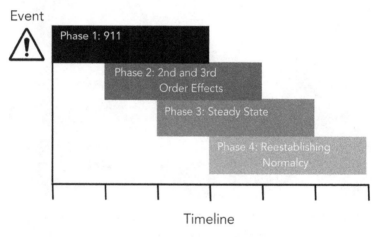

Over time, the crisis response evolves through the four phases. Each phase overlaps, demonstrating that not all aspects of a crisis will be at the same phase line simultaneously.

- Phase 1—The 911 Moment

- Phase 2—Second and Third Order Effects

- Phase 3—The Steady State

- Phase 4—Reestablishing Normalcy

As we go through the phases, we'll look at them from a few different crises so you can see how disasters evolve, no matter the scale. You may start to recognize familiar events happening around you even as you read this.

Welcome to the anatomy of a crisis.

PHASE 1—THE 911 MOMENT

The moment a crisis begins, you enter an emergency mindset. The status quo has been upended by an unexpected event, activity, or evolution. You suddenly pivot to a whole new problem set, and under immense pressure and uncertainty. It is an overwhelming moment that requires immediate action to save lives, prepare for major changes, and address fears.

This phase can vary in length depending on the scope of the crisis. If you cut yourself while preparing dinner, the 911 moment begins with the first drop of blood and ends the moment you've stopped the bleeding. The 911 moment for a natural disaster generally lasts as long as the event itself. For a startup, that 911 moment could last until you've attained some manner of revenue balance. You have to be prepared to endure whatever happens next.

The most important aspect of entering a crisis is understanding your role as a leader. You can't just sit back and play observer; you need to make tough decisions for the greater good. Remember, you're holding this book right now because you understand the need to find your end game. This isn't a how-to for waiting on others to solve your problems. That book was a few aisles down.

Have you ever sensed an impending accident? Or watched a storm form overhead? Crises are sudden, but they don't always appear out of nowhere. Identifying the signs enables you to prepare and plan. However, you can't rely on predictions or instincts.

Geologists and seismologists are able to make predictions, but tectonic plates don't follow strict rules. In the same vein, meteorologists can look at the data and make decent predictions about the weather, but they aren't always accurate.

Once the 911 moment begins, you'll find yourself reacting to any number of challenges. This is when you need to trust your instincts, and your preparations, as you endure the initial chaos. Even with proper planning, this can be a difficult phase. Emotions run high, teams grow anxious, and unpredictable turns can come at any time.

Information is a powerful currency. In the first phase of a crisis, you need to distinguish between information (raw) and intelligence (analyzed) and to take all new information with a grain of salt.

Discordant information abounds in chaos. This means you need to carefully curate your sources of information. The unfortunate side effect of access to all of this raw data is an entire ecosystem of unintentional—or often extremely deliberate—misinformation.

In a crisis, accepting incorrect intel as gospel can have devastating consequences. If you're running a business and follow a bad tip, you can lose large amounts of money. If you're in a life or death situation, the consequences are far more tragic.

In the initial weeks of COVID-19, information changed almost hourly. First, masks were a priority, then washing hands, then sanitizing everything, then masks *weren't* working, then certain medications were recommended, and so on. If you tried to make sense of the raw data, it would almost seem like no one knew what they were doing. Some media personalities amplified misinformation, and now you have a medical crisis compounded by a distrustful public. The truth was that the science of managing COVID-19 was updated along with the arrival of new data. Scientists and immunologists wanted to provide the best, most up-to-date information possible. However, the average citizen didn't understand that the constant changes were just part of the scientific process, and they grew frustrated. Complex problems can't often be packaged in simple ways without losing accuracy.

So how do you vet your sources? We'll cover that in a later chapter, as we want to be thorough in analyzing our intelligence.

As a leader, you will be called upon to make incredibly tough decisions under pressure, and some of those choices won't be the right ones. That's okay. So long as you don't freeze, so long as you work to keep your team moving, you are surviving. That's what matters at this moment. But what happens once the chaos ends?

PHASE 2—SECOND AND THIRD ORDER EFFECTS

In the world of emergency medicine, there is something called the "golden hour." Coined around the First World War, doctors found that patients of traumatic injury stood a higher chance of survival if they received proper medical attention within sixty minutes of the event. Phase 1 of a crisis is that golden hour. But once the patient is stable, once a disaster has run its course, the danger isn't over. Now it's time to look for the second and third effects of a calamity. Welcome to Phase 2.

Imagine a tornado sweeps through a town. The initial danger is, obviously, the vortex of wind and debris that can injure or kill. People bunker down and wait out the storm. When the storm ends, however, the danger isn't over.

The tornado ran through power lines, causing a major blackout that will require significant time and money to repair. Roads are covered in debris, meaning emergency services will have trouble making it to those in need. A town of a few thousand people is now displaced and needs shelter and supplies. These are the follow-on effects of the storm.

Second and third effects can be devastating if not properly addressed. The floods in Pakistan brought in outside contaminants and germs, so one of Mike's first issues was water sanitation—but he also needed to educate the refugees on procedures to keep them safe from dysentery. Mike had to be wary of another crisis brewing in the midst of his current one, all while making decisions that led toward his end game.

A key characteristic of Phase 2 is that none of these solutions are permanent. You are making decisions that move you forward, but they are not the final word on the situation. As a leader, you need to realize when a fix is actually just a bandage. Stopping the bleeding on your cut finger with a towel is not nearly the same as sutures and gauze.

Phase 2 is marked by moving from *reacting* to *acting*. You now have a bit more time and space to make deliberate decisions, all centered around your end game. You move from an emergency mindset to a recovery mindset. At this point, maybe you've gained enough clients and steady work that you have the capital to survive for a few years. This means you can look further into the future and enact bolder plans.

Some solutions also bring new problems. That's part and parcel for this phase of a crisis. The decisions you make as a leader might plug one leak while creating another. You can't get discouraged by cascading events, but you need to be aware that they can happen. Always try to lead in a manner that anticipates these follow-on considerations before they become problems.

What does this mean for you? As a leader, your job doesn't end. Full stop. You are always "on." The quality of your decisions has to remain high because most everything rides on your sense of direction. You'll also need to observe and review the information that is available so you can make informed decisions.

At this stage of the crisis, accurate information is a little easier to come by. You still have to vet your sources and defer to experts when possible. It may not be your usual style to ignore your gut and listen to someone else, but a crisis requires a bit of open-mindedness and a lot of challenged perspectives.

With all you're taking in, you'll want to establish meetings with your team to discuss what has happened in the business, with your clients, with your competition, and how you are going to move forward toward your end game. In the military, these are Battle Update Briefs or Commander's Update Brief—or BUBs and CUBs if you like acronyms. Each leader has a chance to give a succinct update, share their plan, and get immediate feedback.

As with any crisis, the major effects will slowly fade. The floodwaters recede, the ground stops shaking, and the fires die out. If you cut your hand and needed stitches, Phase 2 ends when you arrive home from the hospital. The damage is there, but you've fixed the structural issues, and you are ready to continue with your normal work day. However, "normal" hasn't returned just yet.

Even after you've addressed the logistic issues and put new plans in place to move toward your end game, you're not out of the woods. Welcome to Phase 3, the steady state.

PHASE 3—THE STEADY STATE

There is a phrase that is thrown around a lot during the aftermath of any disaster: The New Normal. It means accepting a new world, a new status quo. For COVID-19, it meant wearing a mask when traveling or entering some places of business. For the Pakistani flood victims, it meant living in camps while awaiting the rebuilding of their homes. For a business, it could mean working without a dedicated office space, or employees doubling up on duties to keep overhead low.

Pakistan Army-administered refugee camp in the Northwest Frontier province of Pakistan.

Phase 3 is a steady state of being, but it is not a sustainable environment. Or rather, it can't be a *self-sustainable* environment. The steady state is marked by reestablishing some semblance of routine that allows some degree of reset. Your employees will start taking time off again, the bizarre will seem familiar, and you can almost imagine continuing this way forever. It's important to recognize that you aren't out of the disaster just yet.

As Pakistan's ground began to dry after the flooding, engineering teams set to work rebuilding the infrastructure. Roads had to be repaired, power had to be reconnected.

During that time, refugees couldn't simply return home. Sometimes, those homes no longer existed. Other times, they were simply unfit for human habitation. People were suddenly without work, which necessitated supply operations to ensure people had their basic needs met. Work programs were established in coordination with the Pakistani government so people could continue to make money and assist in the rebuilding effort. Many of these new workers were a major part of the Phase 2 logistic effort, converting an untamed area of land into a livable region for tens of thousands of people.

The most important point to remember is that Phase 3 will end. The steady state can lull you into a sense of routine, but you can't lose focus. You can still make decisions and take actions that move you toward your end goals.

As a leader, you also need to watch for signs of burnout in your team during this phase. During the recovery operations in Pakistan, similar to WWII leadership tactics, Mike cycled his troops from the front lines to areas in the back to rest and recover. Wading through a destroyed country day after day creates a huge mental burden, and it's easy to lose sight of any good that's happening. During the first two phases, adrenaline levels are high and support seems endless. As the crisis fades from public memory, those at the center can feel very isolated. This is a time when mental health should absolutely be a focus.

Finally, plan your exit. At this point in the crisis, you'll see the finish line not far in the distance. It's time to dismantle the emergency infrastructure and prepare for Phase 4.

PHASE 4—REESTABLISHING NORMALCY

The biggest decision that a leader has to make in Phase 4 is **announcing that the crisis is over**. This can be a tricky choice because you don't want to call the game too early. A crisis mindset is a very productive one, but at a cost. You can easily overuse that asset and burn out your team. Timing the end of a crisis is as much about knowing the truth of the situation as it is knowing the capabilities of your people.

Destroyed local library. Countrywide, over 10,000 students and 1,850 teachers lost their lives on October 7, 2005, the day of the 7.6 magnitude earthquake, as reported by the Pakistan Army during the Federal Relief Commissions After Action Seminar.

Admiral LeFever presenting the completion plaque to a teacher in the town of Miani Bandi, Pakistan, in Kardala Village. The project included the construction of seven sea-huts for a boys' school and a girls' school in order to allow 400 students to resume classes after their school was decimated in the quake.

Exiting a crisis means returning to a changed world. No matter how much you may want it to, life isn't just going to go back to the way it was. Following a disaster, people change. Priorities change. Infrastructure changes. That's why your end game needs to take that evolution into consideration. Just as the world now exists in the aftermath of the crisis, so must you. Things have changed, and you need to change with them.

As recovery finished in Pakistan, Mike saw the country reestablish a normal way of life. Farms picked up production and replanted lost fields. The task force ended delivery of supplies.

Homes were rebuilt and occupied, schools resumed, and life returned. It was a coordinated timeline with no surprises to the Pakistan government nor military in defining the end of disaster and moving on to reconstruction.

The "no surprises" was part of the end game strategy. Mike knew that—once the crisis was over—they needed to leave Pakistan to run itself again. He wanted to build relationships even as they were rebuilding the country. Sure, it was time to leave, but they had changed minds along the way. The steady state was over, and it was time to move forward.

When you're running a startup, exiting the steady state usually comes with expansion. You have the capital and capability to hire on a larger team, lightening the load across the board. Now you're able to grow your business without burdening your team. Even though more is getting done and more money is coming in, the actual workload feels more manageable. The decisions you made all brought you to this point. This is your end game, at least for this phase of your business.

Phase 4 is short, but it's not ripping off a Band-Aid—you don't want to do anything that could risk backsliding. You will make quick decisions that take you out of the old mindset and into a more relaxed posture. Most importantly, you shouldn't go into this phase without having planned for it throughout the crisis.

Knowing your end date is as important as knowing your end game, and that timeline might not be visible early on in the crisis. In the same sense, you as a leader need to keep that macro perspective in mind when moving through your phases.

Your end game will look radically different from that of other organizations. What will work for you might not work for another. COVID-19 restrictions in rural states vastly differed from those in more populous areas, and the country didn't go through the four phases at the same speed. It is also important to remember that you can't force a crisis to move faster. If your end date becomes a moving target, that isn't a failure. It just means you need to demonstrate flexibility.

Leaving a crisis can also mean stumbling, but that isn't always the same as backsliding. When Mike left Pakistan the second time, there were areas where supplies ran low or times when a water purifier failed. When you exit your own crisis, you might stumble as well. Your startup might have a lean period, or a client might leave, or an employee might quit. This doesn't mean you've failed; it means you're adapting to the new reality.

As time passes, memory of the crisis fades. You often forget the worst parts of your time in that space and in that mindset. That's why it is critical to take a moment and document the aftermath. Look at the lessons learned, of the measures that worked and those that didn't. Be brutally honest about how you and your team performed under the harshest circumstances. That way, in the future, you will have a guide to manage the next crisis.

The more you study how things went, the better prepared you will be down the road. After a hurricane, meteorologists spend countless hours examining everything that happened before and after the storm. City planners identify where flooding occurred and implement new designs to prevent damage in the future. Governments examine what measures helped save lives and where they fell short in protecting their communities.

THE ANATOMY OF A CRISIS

Understanding the anatomy of a crisis is step one. As a leader, you need to be prepared for how these phases are managed and take the actions needed to reach your desired end game. While there is no single checklist that can prepare you for every possible scenario, knowing the tools you need to weather the storm makes you more likely to survive.

- Phase 1—The 911 Moment. React to the chaos and put out the fires. A strong plan will serve you well here, and keep you moving into Phase 2.

- Phase 2—Second and Third Order Effects. What new issues were created by the initial disaster? Make plans and solve problems, but angle yourself toward your end game.

- Phase 3—The Steady State. Find your routine and develop your exit strategy.

- Phase 4—Reestablishing Normalcy. Exit the crisis into your end game and move on to the next chapter.

Just as a doctor understands human anatomy in order to better perform their job, you should understand the anatomy of a crisis so you can better do yours.

THE WATERS RISING

The toll of the floods was great, but could have been far worse. Fortunately, only 1,677 lives were lost, but over 17 million people were affected. Over one million homes were gone, with ten million displaced citizens in need of support. Using the knowledge gained from the previous disaster, they were able to overcome the worst of this crisis.

When Mike was in Pakistan to fight the floods, he found himself in a very familiar world. Though he had a new team and a new problem, the mission remained the same. The phases of the crisis progressed just like before, and the decisions he made helped take him and the people of Pakistan to a desired end game.

It wasn't that Mike didn't feel any stress during the ordeal. Far from it; a crisis is a very stressful experience. However, he was able to call upon all the lessons learned from the earthquake to address this new disaster. Having that knowledge built confidence and allowed him to make tough decisions without the fear of what might happen. It enabled him to *lead*, and that's the most important thing a leader can do.

One of the best assets you can have in a crisis is a strong, well-assembled team. The right group of people can manage all aspects of a crisis, allowing you to do the important work of making decisions that lead to the end game. This isn't always the archetypes you'll find in your normal office space, but rather a set of skills that you'll need to identify in people.

It's time to build your battle staff.

CHAPTER 3

BUILDING
A TEAM

Mike had spent decades learning and growing as a leader. He trained in naval tactics, combined arms operations, and joint task force deployments. Throughout this journey, he had gained a sense for people, learning how to read them and their abilities. It was a key skill for building a battle staff.

In the history of the US Navy, Mike was only the second commander to field the Expeditionary Strike Group ONE. Though he certainly had time leading ships on deployment, the variety of personnel and equipment meant he needed specific experts to lead each group, and he would be fully reliant on their knowledge and advice. Along with his personal command group, he had intelligence officers, Explosive Ordnance Disposal specialists (EOD), engineers, SEALs, and experts for aviation, construction, and medical. Some of these commissioned officers and noncommissioned officers (NCO) had passed through his commands before, and others were brand new faces with untapped potential. By the time they deployed, Mike felt confident he had the right group to face for expected missions.

And then the mission changed.

When the call came to switch from a Ready Force to the humanitarian mission in Pakistan for the earthquake, Mike's first thought was to prepare his staff. This was a radical change in the expected mission, and not everyone was capable of demonstrating such flexibility. Still, Mike knew the people on his team and trusted them with autonomy.

After receiving the new orders, Mike met with his team and discussed what would happen next. They had to conduct swift battle handoffs with their subordinates so that the original mission could move forward, all while drafting up new operation orders for the humanitarian expedition. There was no time for the usual rounds of planning and discussion. They had to come up with a feasible, workable solution in the fourteen hours it would take to travel to the country. This was a crisis. Mike needed to identify the right traits to build an austere staff.

Admiral LeFever and BG Mike Nagata surveying the affected areas in the north after the flood of 2010.

With a disaster like an earthquake, some of the roles seem obvious. Medical experts are needed to determine and establish the health needs of the survivors. Engineers are needed to repair buildings, roads, and infrastructure. Aviation experts are needed to coordinate the heavy lift for supplies and rescue operations. Ground troops are needed for manual labor, search and rescue, and security. Mike also knew that intel on the ground would be chaotic, so he needed the right people to source and validate information.

With a hasty plan discussed, Mike went to grab a few minutes' rest before his flight to Bahrain and the long flight into Pakistan. His mind was focused, ready for anything, but his stomach was twisted. There's only so much a leader can do before it all comes down to the action on the ground.

The team Mike selected came with years of training and experience, but he looked beyond their titles and resumes. He brought a planning officer—a Marine colonel—who had an inquisitive and organized mind. He was also studying for his PhD and came across as a thoughtful leader. His Intelligence Officer, another Marine, had demonstrated a unique ability to quickly analyze and decipher information, a critical skill for the coming mission. EOD and SEAL teams operated autonomously, often in small teams under ten people. With so much ground to cover, that confidence and skill set would be a game changer. He brought experts in military construction and mobile hospitals.

As they touched down into the alien world of a ravaged Pakistan, this was a team he had trained with during workups—but they had never trained for anything like this.

A TEAM TO ENDURE A CRISIS

A strong, diverse team is instrumental in navigating a crisis. But if you can't know what's coming down the road, how do you build the right team? The answer is that you can focus on the inherent skills of your team rather than specific job titles. There are key roles to fill during any crisis, and you can probably fill them all without opening your rolodex.

Each business has its own subject matter experts that are required for a successful company. You can't exactly start a law practice without lawyers or a medical office without doctors.

However, a crisis might not need those specific professions. Instead, a crisis requires levels of management in logistics, operations, communication, and information gathering. You need to learn who is capable of filling which roles, including yourself.

Understand that in a crisis, you cannot work alone. You may be a mentally tough and competent person, but you cannot do everything at once. As Mike began Phase 1 in Pakistan, he needed team members that could operate autonomously, leaving him the freedom to look at the big picture and formulate an end game.

The team you build for a crisis isn't going to magically come from thin air. You likely won't see a crisis coming, so you're going to be entering the first phase only with those around you. These are the people you work with, the people you live with. These are the cards you're dealt, and you have to find the strengths in that team.

Your small business may have a killer PR guy, but now a crisis has you pivoting to a completely new market. How will this person react? Are their contacts still usable? What about your logistics teams? If your business faced a shutdown due to quarantine, how would that affect your ability to meet customer needs? Is your team prepared to adapt and overcome the challenges on the horizon?

When Concentric realized its international business was about to be blocked off, it was important to create the right climate within the organization. As leaders, it was Mike and Roderick's responsibility to ensure the culture inside the company reflected a confident and positive outlook. They needed to empower their staff, help everyone recognize that this was a challenge they would overcome.

The only person you'll know intimately is yourself, and a crisis might reveal things that you *didn't* know. While we all like to think of ourselves as the heroes of the story, sometimes we are best serving as supporting roles. As we go through each avatar and discuss what they bring to the team, it's important that you remove your ego. Don't expect to be great at everything, and admit when you're not. As a leader, you can't do every single job. You need to identify your own limitations along with what needs to get done.

For each avatar, we are going to break down the discussion into key components:

- What this role is for

- How to recognize this role within a person

- What tasks are suitable for this role

- How to utilize them best

- How to recognize if you fit this role

THE DIPLOMAT
What They Are

The Diplomat is the key player in your end game. They are relationship guru. Every office has one or two people just like this. They can talk to anyone about any subject and come across as genial and approachable. They make connections on instinct, build bridges before their second cup of coffee, secure deals that shouldn't be possible. This is the person who calls back the on-the-fence client and secures the deal with just a few sentences. They know the vendors on a first-name basis, and they spend time with the competition so they can keep track of opportunities.

These are negotiators, leaders that pull people together and often act as a moderator in a heated discussion. They have soft skills on top of their soft skills and can make any scenario sound good. They are the Michael Jordan of diplomacy.

In a crisis, you'll need to interact with a lot of different people and organizations in order to pursue your end game. The diplomat shouldn't just be a schmoozer; they actually need to know what they're talking about. They provide accurate information to the right people so you can gain access to the resources you need.

This can be a PR manager in your business, the J6 (Communications Officer) of a military unit, or the press secretary of a government. However, this person doesn't need to come from a communications background; they just need to show off the right traits in order to serve this role in your crisis team.

Recognizable Traits

A Diplomat is confident, but they need humility. Arrogance is a relationship killer—especially during a crisis—just as confidence is key. If you're a titan of the industry, you can rely on people's desire for access for only so long. If you're a smaller team struggling through a crisis, burning bridges can be a death bell.

Patience is a vital trait for just about everyone, but especially so for the Diplomat. They are going to be organizing the internal to the external and vice versa, and often that means a lot of waiting around for other departments to take action. All throughout that downtime, they need to be building relationships. That's where empathy can be a key trait as well. Diplomats often need to place themselves in the mindset of the other side, demonstrating understanding and compassion when tempers are high.

Of course, it all comes back to the end game. The actions they take and the statements they make should all be focused on delivering you to the end game. That means knowing how to organize their time and tasks day to day, strengthening relationships under the worst circumstances, and remaining a positive face for the company.

Required Tasks

During any crisis, there are numerous resources that you will need in order to survive. The specifics depend on the type of crisis. During the earthquake, Mike needed medical supplies and food rations and material for shelters, let alone the normal equipment required for vehicle maintenance. A strong Diplomat greases the logistic tracks so those resources are (hopefully) never hard to find.

They may need to speak with the press and answer difficult questions or explain your choices. If this was a large car accident and you were in charge of the scene, you would select an officer with strong social skills to cordon off the onlookers and deliver a simple message to the press until an official statement was ready.

Diplomats might need to negotiate contracts with vendors now that the crisis has changed your needs. They'll let your clients know that you are still open for business, and they'll seek out new revenue streams in the process.

Anywhere that a soft skill is required, the Diplomat appears.

How to Utilize Them Best

This is fairly simple. The Diplomat manages relationships with outside sources. You don't need the Diplomat focused on internal morale or corporate strategy. They shouldn't be bogged down with anything that doesn't directly support the end game. They do need to be tied in with logistics, but only so far as it applies to communication with vendors or clients.

Once you've found the right person, you also want to empower them as a communicator. They need to have guidelines about what to say and who to prioritize, but you don't need to micro-manage your Diplomat. You want them to feel comfortable acting autonomously.

How to Recognize If You Are the Diplomat

If you're the person who is always ready to have the hard conversation, you are the Diplomat. Soft skills can be learned and grown over time, but a crisis is not the right moment to try something new. If you aren't comfortable being the center of attention, with people hanging on your every word, this won't be the role for you.

However, if you are often the cheerleader of your team, sing-ing their praises to anyone that will listen, this could be your role in the crisis. It's important that you train to focus on the specific tasks we mentioned, but as a leader your role will likely be expanded. If the Diplomat is a subordinate, they can focus entirely on building relationships and coordination. If you take on this responsibility, you'll also need to build in time to communicate with your team and ensure the organization is headed in the same direction.

Once you recognize who on your team is taking this role, support them and stay out of their way. They need to under-stand the scope of their responsibilities, the importance of their role, and the limits for expression. After that, trust them to accomplish their tasks.

Admiral LeFever meets with US Ambassador to Pakistan Ryan Crocker with his J2 (Intelligence Lead) and J6 (Military version of CIO) representatives at Relief Operations at Chaklala Air Base in Islamabad, Pakistan.

In Pakistan, Mike worked with Ambassador Ryan Crocker, a career diplomat who had worked in the organization for decades. While not THE Diplomat (by official US Department of State title) of Mike's team, Ambassador Crocker's leadership and deep expertise in the area was invaluable. Ambassador Crocker knew the movers and shakers of Pakistan, how they needed to be handled in order to accept the help of the US military, and where to push to gain the right resources. He also had an innate understanding of the culture of the area, which proved a boon for Mike when his drive to build and lead threatened to create some friction. Ambassador Crocker was also incredible at maneuvering through the US Interagency as well!

The Diplomat is a key member of your crisis team. Once you've identified them, trust that they will serve as a faithful representative of your company.

THE CONDUCTOR
What They Are

During a crisis, someone has to keep things moving. Time, as we previously mentioned, is a precious commodity. You have to keep the train running on time. If any department falls behind, you'll lose momentum catching them up. That can cause you to miss your deadlines, lose sight of your end game, and even backslide to previous phases. For all those reasons, you need to find your Conductor.

They might be a Chief of Staff or a COO or a mid-level manager. This is the person that the class always turned to when it was time to organize by height, last names, or birth dates. They track data as a hobby and can walk you through the cause and effect of a decision with painstaking detail. They are often in the leadership position, since so much of what they do is front and center of an organization.

It's not just about getting subordinates to work on their tasks, but to keep all departments at the same pace. If logistics get too far ahead, supplies will start to pile up unused. If marketing goes rogue, supply won't be able to meet demand. The Conductor ensures that the team moves forward equally and efficiently until they reach the end game.

When Mike went to manage the Pakistan earthquake, his Marine planning officer served as the Conductor. He knew Mike's schedule to the minute, and he made sure they stuck to it no matter what. As time went on, Mike's reliance on the Conductor allowed him to look more and more at the big picture of their humanitarian mission. It took major tactical decisions off his plate and helped keep the team on track.

This is a critical position, so how do you find them?

Recognizable Traits

Without question, the Conductor needs to have exceptional organizational skills. This isn't the person that puts "organized and task-oriented" on a resume. This is the person that lists their qualifications in descending order of importance based on the position to which they've applied. This is someone with zero missed tick marks on their daily to-do list. They stick to a schedule with strict discipline and ensure others do the same. They Get Stuff Done!

Organization isn't just a personality quirk; it's a passion. The Conductor uses spreadsheets to plan family vacations and birthday parties. When you ask them for a food recommendation, they know which restaurants have their primary chefs working on particular days.

A Conductor is laser-focused on logistics as well. They are rarely short of an item when working on a project. They don't have to search for the last puzzle piece because they've already organized them by shape and size. In a crisis, the Conductor is going to research supply lines whether you ask them or not. They have someone on the ground in the Suez Canal watching for blockages. They have the personal numbers for the warehouse managers of your most often-needed supplies.

Most of all, the Conductor has an internal clock that never runs slow. If you give them a deadline, it will be hit. It's a guarantee. This would be a great employee on any day of the week, but they are champions during a crisis. You will gain a newfound respect for their abilities, and your company will thrive due to their efforts.

One important thing to note about Conductors is that they might not *appear* like the ideal candidate on the outside. What we mean is, don't judge a book by its cover. They may have the messiest desk in the office, but they can find anything for you at a second's notice. They never miss a deadline, and they keep others on track.

Required Tasks

In a crisis, you need critical thinking skills and the ability to visualize a plan from inception to fruition. The Conductor excels in this area. If you have a task that needs completing, they can tell you how to do it, which logistic chains are needed, and where the resources will be spent. They aren't necessarily the best at planning out a task, but they are the best at connecting the necessary people together and keeping the work on schedule.

Conductors will have a hand in logistics, as managing supply lines is a critical part of completing work on time. They'll likely interact with your information gatherers, taking the processed data and working it into their solutions so you are always ahead of any issues. The Conductor knows that a major event is happening downtown, so all supply routes need to avoid certain roads at certain times.

Conductors are great subordinate leaders and executive officers, leading teams with the discretion of the big boss. If you need to focus on another area, or if you are better suited in another role, this person keeps the rest of the team on track. Time management can mean the difference between success and failure, and this person gets the job done.

In Pakistan, as Mike's team grew larger and larger, he saw elements of his crisis staff spread throughout different departments. He had a dedicated officer for managing the flight lines. With helicopters and planes coming and going at a steady pace, someone needed to take charge and focus solely on that area. Mike had an aviation expert planning the flight lists and coordinating with efforts on the ground, and the planning officer ensured that this expert remained in sync with the task force's timeline.

Over the course of the next few months, the aviation officer developed a team of his own, with a Conductor handling things within the department. In fact, each organization began to separate into a similar breakdown of roles and responsibilities. You could walk through any group of people and quickly pick out their avatar. For Mike, it was a light-bulb moment. He saw how these personalities naturally rise

during a crisis, and he was proud to see his leaders recognizing the versatility of their staff.

How to Utilize Them Best

A Conductor, above all else, helps you accomplish your goals.
In order to utilize them best, you need to provide them with
accurate and specific tasks and deadlines. They are fairly
autonomous, but you will need to ensure that everyone in your
organization recognizes their authority. When you're not in
the room, does the Conductor speak with your voice? Do others
respect their orders? It does you no good to have an organized
second-in-command if they can't get anyone to follow.

At the beginning of the crisis, when you've identified this
person and set them to work, watch the timeline. If tasks are
completed according to schedule, the Conductor is working
right. Verify work from time to time so you can be confident in
everyone's ability, but build that trust out until you are confident in your team. If the Conductor is truly effective, you'll
be able to walk away from that aspect of management for the
duration of the crisis. You'll still need to be involved, providing
the plans and deadlines, but you'll have developed competent
leadership in your team.

How to Recognize If You Are the Conductor

If you are the taskmaster, are organized, and *need* to be the
one holding people accountable, then this role may well be for

you. Often in smaller teams, the leader *has to be* the Conductor. There are no real mid-level managers in small companies. Coworkers are less likely to recognize their peers as suddenly being in charge. That means you'll need to take on this role in order to ensure work flows correctly.

As your company grows, however, you may find it takes too much of your time to play the Conductor. There are macro concerns that have to be taken into account during any crisis, and you'll burn out if you wear too many hats. However, if you feel more comfortable in this role, it just means you'll need to delegate other responsibilities to other subordinate leaders in your organization.

Regardless of who becomes the Conductor, make it clear to the rest of the team that this person acts at the behest of the leader. Empowerment is nothing without authority.

THE MAVERICK
What They Are

In a free-flowing discussion, the fundamental of design thinking is to evaluate all ideas equally. However, there are often those people that seem to be operating on a different plane. They come up with outlandish options, sometimes comically bad, and yet they always seem to find a thread that leads to the proper solution.

This is the Maverick, and they might just be your most valuable player.

Mavericks think outside the box as a rule. It's not just that they come up with radical ideas; they think about the world in a way you just don't. They help break your train of thought so you can pull the pieces together.

Have you ever had a problem that you just couldn't solve? No matter how many angles you took, it remained an elusive target. Then one day, in the shower, the inspiration just hit. Suddenly you saw the big picture and how everything fit together. It was because you'd taken your mind off of all your old ideas and allowed it to think objectively. That's what a Maverick does.

This person might not be your best employee, but they get the job done. If you shadowed them for a day, you'd probably be offended by their work habits. They take breaks at odd times, approach problems at odd angles, and infuriatingly accomplish their tasks as ordered. You likely keep them on a very short leash. However, in a crisis, this next-level thinking is a huge boon.

A crisis requires, among a host of other things, flexibility. It requires looking at a problem and coming up with a solution to a *totally different* problem, then finding a way to work that back to the original. It's 3D chess, and a Maverick loves to play against the odds.

When Concentric faced the loss of nearly half its revenue, it took a Maverick to approach the problem with a radical solution. The pivot to domestic companies was fairly obvious, but introducing a massive digitization of the business seemed crazy. Mike and Roderick didn't plan the company to run webinars and virtual symposiums, nor to monitor COVID-19 protocol assurance by cruise goers, but the demand was there. Concentric's Maverick found an untapped niche that supported the company's mission.

Mavericks often get a bad reputation, especially in larger teams. They can be loners or prefer to stick with a small group of like-minded people. In Pakistan, those were Mike's EOD and SEAL teams members. By their very nature, these groups operated in small units, sometimes as few as three or four. In the midst of a humanitarian crisis, that kind of effort just wouldn't make a dent. However, Mike found that these teams often had to think radically in order to find a solution that was manageable for a smaller team.

When he came across an issue that seemed to stump his leaders, he would toss it to the SEALs and EOD officers. Of course, he provided a commander's intent and boundaries so they didn't go completely off the rails. After a few hours, the team leaders would return with a few harebrained ideas...and one that just might work.

The Maverick is your "break glass in case of emergency" employee. During a crisis, it's time to take them out of the box and put them to work.

Recognizable Traits

We might have been a bit harsh on this character from the start, but your Maverick isn't a loose cannon. You'll find this person by listening to how they approach a problem.

Mavericks are outside-the-box thinkers. They tend to work independently, preferring to pursue a goal at their own pace and direction. They might not be strict on deadlines, but they can be wrangled into one. They often have a creative streak; maybe they are artists on the side.

They might seem low energy during a normal workday, and then suddenly they perk up when there is a challenging problem to solve. These are people that seek out the unsolvable, even if they never find the solution.

They can rub their coworkers and managers the wrong way at times. Others might not see them as valuable, radical thinkers, but rather as disruptive and disorganized. Their tendency toward bursts of productivity can lead them to burn bright and to burn out.

Required Tasks

When you need a solution to a radical problem, call a radical thinker. This is your everything-tool, the person that you wind up and point at a challenge. When a crisis requires flexibility and quick thinking, you're going to want your Maverick.

At the beginning of COVID-19, Concentric needed to take months of scheduled in-person meetings and convert them to virtual conferences. While some of the team were familiar with Skype and Zoom, no one really knew how they were going to be able to have quality conversations with clients unless they could be in the same room. Mike and Roderick called upon a Maverick in their team to come up with a solution.

Like so many companies, they turned to Microsoft Teams and now Google Meet, but the Maverick didn't stop there. They put together a plan to quickly bring their clients up to speed on the new process, to make everything run smoothly. While it seems like a small thing, it helped reinforce confidence in their customer base. It kept the doors open, and sometimes that is all you need.

Mavericks encourage you to take risks, and they are the ones that can quickly write up risky plans. In a crisis, nothing is guaranteed. You are going to make decisions that may lead you in the wrong direction. You'll make mistakes. But the worst thing you can do is try to avoid all risks, because you simply can't. Instead, you need to take calculated risks that lead you toward your end game. A Maverick is an excellent avatar to sort out what risks lay in your path.

How to Utilize Them Best

A Maverick, more than any other avatar, needs guardrails. They have a tendency to cross the lines and get out of their work areas, which can rub coworkers the wrong way. While you want them thinking radically and creatively, you don't want them assuming other people's roles and distracting from the job at hand.

You might need to caution them before large meetings so they don't say something out of turn. The Maverick is the person that calls out the emperor for wearing no clothes. While that may be the kind of thinking you need, it's not what you want to happen in a critical meeting with a client or vendor.

Things you don't think you need to say to other employees... you need to say to the Maverick.

At the same time, you want to loosen the reins and allow the Maverick to explore. They need the ability to see a bit of the big picture, and they absolutely need to understand the end game. This enables them to think critically about solutions to problems you might not have foreseen. Use Mavericks as a sounding board, and listen when they chase ideas that might seem a bit outside your comfort zone.

If properly utilized, a Maverick will be one of your best assets during a crisis.

How to Recognize If You Are the Maverick

As a leader, you can play that role. Part of your responsibility as the head of an organization is finding a path forward. That can often mean radical decisions and pivots. Mike's experience in the military taught him that a leader needs a plan and the flexibility to adapt. Remember, if it's stupid and it works, it wasn't stupid.

If you're a Maverick, you *must* surround yourself with people who are not. You need steady leaders to tug on your reins if you veer too far off course. That can be a huge challenge, since you're going to need to drop all ego during a crisis and trust your team. If you have a team of Mavericks, you can find yourself overwhelmed by chaos.

A good example would be Steve Jobs. He was a Maverick, looking at the tech world almost from the outside. His solutions to home computing, music, and cell phones seemed outlandish and radical at the time. However, if you know anything about his professional history, this mindset didn't always serve him or the company well. His greatest successes came with the help of opposite-minded people surrounding him and honing his ideas into workable solutions.

It is more than likely that you have Maverick tendencies, especially if you're running a startup. Leaders, by nature, think a little differently. Despite this, you'll often identify others that fit this role better than you, so you can focus on a different specialty.

THE GENERALIST
What They Are

We want to clarify a phrase that is often misunderstood: jack-of-all-trades, master of none. It seems to imply that someone with a bit of skill in many areas is less worthy than a specialist. Aside from being only half the original quote, it's also wildly incorrect. The full phrase, by the way, is "A jack-of-all-trades is a master of none, but oftentimes better than a master of one." In most startups, and even in large established businesses, you need Swiss Army knives. You need employees that can handle a multitude of areas. In a crisis, this is even more important. You hire employees based on specific skill sets, all centered around your business model. However, people aren't just tools; they have interests on the side, previous jobs with vastly different focuses, and they'll likely be able to fill any number of other positions. In a crisis, you need to identify these Generalists as soon as you can.

As you've seen from previous examples, a crisis can demand a major pivot for your organization. You might have built a team for one task, but now you need to work in another area of the field. The Specialist won't be as flexible, but the Generalist has dozens of skills to call upon in this situation. Suddenly, their varied background is the very thing you need.

A Generalist is a collector of hobbies. They're the art director that builds their own furniture, or the corporate lawyer that writes and directs musical theater. At the office, they could be the IT technician who fixed an issue with the payroll spreadsheet, or the plumber who also is a licensed electrician and HVAC tech. While they don't have mastery of one specific area, they can be placed into a role and succeed. During a crisis, that is exactly the sort of person you need.

A crisis demands change, and you'll often find yourself creating roles without a specific person in mind. This is where the Generalist becomes invaluable. It's not that they always have that specific skill set ready to go, but they are willing to learn on the job and get to a level of proficiency that supports the team.

Will they end up as good as a Specialist in that area? No, of course not. But in a crisis, and often in regular times, a Generalist will perform the job to your satisfaction.

Recognizable Traits

In every office, there is the go-to employee. No matter the task—we need a PowerPoint presentation for a client, we need to set up a conference with four different organizations, we need to do a budget analysis for a major proposal, we need someone to run the HR-mandated training—this is the person you turn to. They are boldly confident wherever they go.

Their job is probably pretty general, such as a mid-level manager or supervisor. They have a laundry list of occupations on their resume, to the point that you might have once been concerned about their longevity. Job-hopping has a bad connotation, but in this case it was evidence that the employee constantly sought new challenges and skills. Now, all of that effort has created a Generalist that helps keep your operation moving.

In his book *Range: Why Generalists Triumph in a Specialized World*, sports journalist David Epstein writes, "In a world that increasingly incentivizes, even demands, hyperspecialization, we need more...people who start broad and embrace diverse experiences and perspectives while they progress." He refers to the famous tennis player Roger Federer, a whirlwind on the court, who actually started his athletic career playing a wide variety of sports before committing to tennis.

Microsoft founder Bill Gates agreed fervently with David's take, noting that the tech world needed generalists to function. Many engineers chose to specialize early, searching for holes to fill in other companies. Generalists sought out the holes in the market and have the flexibility to move in other directions when the winds change. Bill and David also note that specialists tend to get tunnel vision in their work, focusing only on their specific areas of expertise.

In a crisis, a Generalist is always looking for what needs to be done, and that is a critical skill you need on your team.

Required Tasks

A Generalist, as you can probably infer, can be thrown into pretty much anything. They are smart and inquisitive, so they'll often conduct on-the-job training to bring themselves up to speed. They flourish in an environment where they can flex creative thinking and tie multiple tasks together.

Generalists can work in logistics, but they are better suited in front-line positions and operations. They'll fill in the gaps on teams, ensuring you always have a well-rounded group to attack challenges.

The only areas where a Generalist won't succeed are, as you may have guessed, complex and specialized tasks. Remember that these are not experts, so more specified work will only set them up for failure.

Your Generalists are excellent for running headfirst into a new situation, since they flow around established teams looking for gaps to fill. The solutions they offer will be tried and true, so they're not aiming to replace your Mavericks. In fact, they can be a great partner for that avatar to round out the more radical ideas.

How to Utilize Them Best

In Pakistan, Mike had an EOD officer that specialized in force protection. It seemed like he would only succeed in security or basic operations, but that just wasn't the case. This was a smart, curious officer with an innate ability to process information quickly. No matter where Mike put him, the team succeeded. It was like finding a skeleton key.

It's important for you, as a leader, to recognize when a situation is too specific or specialized for a Generalist to work. The Director of NASA doesn't need to be an astronaut, but they need to understand the roles and responsibilities of each person in the organization. However, the Chief of Medicine at a hospital needs to have specific knowledge in order to be a competent leader.

The Generalist is a good communicator, and often asks questions before you need to push information. This is someone who thrives with clear instructions and minimal guidance; if they need you, they will find you. Unlike your Conductor, you'll want to check in from time to time to verify the quality of the work, but you'll more often find the situation well under control.

In a pinch, a Generalist can fill a Specialist role, but you'll be getting a lower-quality result. This means you have to recognize which problems require a Band-Aid and which require more complex operations. The good news is that most Generalists are humble enough to admit when they have reached their maximum potential in a role. They don't want to fail, nor to see the organization fail, so they'll come to you first. Make sure you've created a culture where that honesty is welcomed and rewarded.

How to Recognize If You Are the Generalist

As the leader of an organization, you are more than likely a Generalist in some sense. You have (hopefully) maturity, you have a clear guide stone for the direction you need to go, and you understand enough about the specific tasks of your business to hire the right people. You are a person who completes tasks and seeks out new opportunities. However, as the leader in a crisis, this can be a difficult role.

You are going to have a number of specific and implied tasks during a crisis. Specific means that you have these challenges listed, or even demanded, to be complete. You need to meet these goals in order to succeed, and they have clear objectives. Implied tasks are the connective tissue in between your specified tasks. They might not necessarily be written down, and they might not have clear end points. However, all of this needs to be accomplished in order for you to be successful.

This means it is harder for you to flow in and out of different roles during a crisis. Someone needs to remain focused on the end game, pushing everyone toward the finish line, and maintaining morale along the way. If you overwhelm yourself with more roles, this means something has to give on the other side.

We don't want to discourage you from wearing a few hats. As a leader, you will undoubtedly be jumping into jobs at a moment's notice to ensure work is completed on time. Just make sure you don't lose sight of the bigger picture because you focused too hard on a single task.

THE SPECIALIST
What They Are

In a crisis, you will need people with specific skill sets, all dependent on your organization and the mission. A Specialist is someone trained for a specific task or trade. This isn't just a surgeon, it's a *heart surgeon*. This isn't a handyman, it's an electrician. This is a job that requires specific training and testing, possibly even licensing. A Specialist cannot be easily replaced, but they also can't do much outside of their specific task.

These are the experts in very specific areas. They cover things that are crucial for managing the crisis. They might already have a skill set for your original mission, but they are the person that knows what to do.

If you understand your business, your crisis, you will find the right specialist.

Recognizable Traits

This person is an expert. They are dedicated and driven to pursue excellence in their chosen field. They are knowledgeable in their area but might be a little lighter in others. They don't have much interest outside their area of expertise, which is why they've spent so much time practicing their field.

These are people recruited for a specific purpose. You didn't hire a secretary only to discover they know how to do brain surgery. This is both the benefit and shortcoming of a Specialist. When you need them for their chosen task, they are the best. The job will get done exactly right, on time, and they might even learn more efficient ways of working as they progress. However, they are not as flexible during a crisis.

This also means that during a crisis, their roles won't change. You can't take your software engineer and flex them over to the accounting department to assist in an audit. These skills don't necessarily mesh. That doesn't mean you need to lose a Specialist, just that you'll likely need to seek one out once you've identified your new mission.

An EOD technician is a very specialized role, yet Mike was able to see the other innate skills in his team during the earthquake. While there was no need for the Specialist in that role, the mindset behind it served the organization well. During a crisis, you might discover that your Specialist is also a gifted socializer, or an expert in logistics. That's why it's important to remember that your team's job titles won't necessarily translate into their crisis roles.

Required Tasks

Mike had trained his team for combat, for blowing things up, and now he was tasked with rebuilding and humanitarian efforts...all with the same personnel. Instead of trying to fit everyone into a position, he looked for the roles needed based on the new mission.

He had medics and physicians in the ESG, all with experience setting up hospitals for combat zones. Those specialized skills worked perfectly for establishing MASH units in a disaster-ravaged Pakistan. Combat engineers know how to build infrastructure and temporary habitation on any terrain, which meant they were essential for the rebuilding effort. Mike didn't look at their job title, but rather what expert skills they possessed.

That is the key when finding tasks for the Specialists already on your team. These are well-trained personnel, so marry them to a task that utilizes their skill and knowledge.

This also means that the required tasks will be situation dependent. If your crisis is a lack of clients, you need a marketing specialist. If your crisis is a major car accident on a highway, you'll need experts in traffic control, vehicle recovery, and city planning. Once you identify the problem that needs to be solved, you will know what Specialist to find.

How to Utilize Them Best

Simply put, give them the runway they need. A specialist doesn't need hand-holding. They don't need you to tell them what to do. All they need is to know the scope of the problem and the desired solution (...end game, per se).

In this way, working with a Specialist is easy. You can rely on their expertise and trust that they will get the job done right. This also means you need to communicate with your Conductor, so they don't annoy the Specialist in the midst of their work but rather keep them on track or focused (or aligned) on the end game.

Specialists often require specific tools, both hardware and software. Make sure you are setting them up with the necessary equipment to perform their jobs. Don't worry, they will tell you what they need. That said, set your expectations with them ahead of time so you don't feel the need to hover around them and monitor their progress. This means clear guidelines and KPIs. Set scheduled checkpoints to measure progress, and let them know the milestones that need to be reported.

As we mentioned before, Specialists can get tunnel vision. They often have a personality that thrives in solitude, and they can work themselves too hard and too long. Keep an eye on them for their well-being, and to make sure they don't burn out.

How to Recognize if You Are the Specialist

If you are an expert in one thing, then that is your specialty. As a leader, you will have to balance your duties to the team and the company alongside your tasks as a Specialist. If you are a surgeon running your own practice, then you are both the leader and the Specialist of the team. You still have to manage your staff, sign paychecks, set goals, and meet with clients to expand your business, alongside actually doing *your* job.

If you run a startup, you likely have a specialized skill that you're using as the foundation of the business. In the early stages of the company, you are going to be pulling double or even triple duty, at least until you can afford a larger team to divide out responsibilities. Just as we said above, you need to pay attention to your workload so you don't burn out.

As you bring in a larger and larger team, you'll notice that you no longer fill that Specialist role. Your time as a leader becomes more valuable than the work you would do as a Specialist. As your surgical practice expands, you hire on additional staff to handle the growing number of patients, until finally you hire new surgeons to handle excess cases. After a while, you stop performing surgery to focus on growing your practice, only taking cases that are of particular interest to you.

Gordon Ramsay is an elite-level cook, but most of his time isn't spent in front of a stove. He's built an empire finding Specialists to lead his restaurants and surrounding himself with a highly competent team.

It's all about time management and recognizing how your time would be best spent to lead to your end game.

THE DEFENDER
What They Are

Every organization has a Defender, and it is usually a role filled by the leader. They are the person who watches over the business and the team with a healthy sense of paranoia. This is the person who looks out for liability issues, seeks out toxicity in the office, and acts as a cheerleader outside of the organization.

In Pakistan, you might assume that the defender was the security force protecting the people on the ground, but that is just an aspect of defense. In this case, the Defender was more concerned with the visibility of the task force, with the safety of outside personnel coming into the country, and with the reputation of the effort with the Pakistani government.

Defenders can also be literal defenders, but that role is often filled by Specialists. If your startup faces constant cyber attacks, you'll have a Specialist brought in to set up security. However, your Defender might be the person talking with journalists to get the correct story out to the industry.

Defenders can also be a bit stubborn when it comes to radical change. They are fiercely supportive of the organization to the point that they don't want to see you step too far outside your comfort zone without a good reason. In this way, they are trying to protect you from stretching too thin, but you may need to rein in their intensity so you can properly pivot in a crisis.

Recognizable Traits

We said a healthy dose of paranoia, and we meant it. As the saying goes, it's not paranoia if they really are out to get you. In a crisis, they *really are* out to get you.

When Mike was in Pakistan, there was a real threat of terrorist activity. Militant groups often seek targets of opportunity, and a crisis offers precious targets such as a refugee camp or a civilian-run medical facility. If you're running a startup, your competition is very real and very interested in seeing you fail. Sometimes, they may even try to speed that along by undercutting your bids or stealing away clients.

This is why a Defender is constantly looking out for the worst-case scenario. They have a pessimistic streak, and it keeps them on their toes. In many cases, this comes from experience. A good Defender has been there and seen it all before.

They recognize the telltale signs of an oncoming problem long before it is right in front of them. They plan out scenarios and explore possible solutions in their downtime. This makes them invaluable when the situation inevitably arrives.

In the American version of *The Office,* Dwight Schrute is constantly the butt of jokes for having contingency plans for outlandishly unlikely scenarios. While this is obviously exaggerated for comedic effect, you actually want people like this in your organization. You want someone to be worried about what *could* happen so that you aren't blindsided by what *does* happen.

At the same time, Defenders need to be controlled. This is a person on a short leash, as they can and will chase after problems rather than staying focused on the end game. You don't want them left to their own devices as that might not be your core mission, especially in a crisis.

Required Tasks

The tasks for a Defender depend on your company, your situation, and your end game. They can be different from day to day, or it could be a singular mission. A company lawyer is a Defender that only focuses on legal liability. If you're losing clients to a competitor, the lawyer isn't suddenly going to focus on that.

Common roles of Defenders include force protection, legal review, finances, and brand analysis. You'll often find leaders in this role, as these are duties of managers and above.

In large retail stores, Defenders can work as loss prevention since that is a constant concern. However, the HR manager is also a Defender, protecting employees and the company from toxic environments and major liabilities. At a hospital, the on-site lawyer protects the doctors from malpractice suits, while the security guard at the front protects both the patients and staff.

Let's return to our restaurateur in the midst of a pandemic. The Defender could be the employee monitoring online reviews to ensure the reputation of the business isn't broken. They evaluate delivery services and respond to issues to maintain customer satisfaction.

How to Utilize Them Best

In a way, everyone at your company is a defender. Everyone plays a role in protecting the organization from threats of one area or another. In a crisis, you have to find Defenders for specific tasks, just as you might need Specialists for specific jobs.

In an aviation unit, every single person is a safety officer. They have the ability to call out safety hazards and shut down the flight line to preserve lives. There is also a dedicated safety officer, tasked with specific duties including building a plan to reduce risk and ensure the mission can still be accomplished. A crisis can include physical danger, depending on the situation. You can't always eliminate risk, but you need to mitigate it.

Defenders should have easy access to leadership so they can share concerns and receive updated guidance. They need to know the end game, but their focus will always be on the security of the company.

If you're working in a specialized field, your Defender could be a compliance officer that ensures your actions always stay above board. This could be a lawyer or just a licensed professional with experience in the area. Again, the way you utilize a Defender depends heavily on the crisis you are in.

How to Recognize If You Are the Defender

If you're the person controlling all the risks in the organization, you are the Defender. It often falls to the leader to take on this role, especially in smaller companies. You clearly have a stake in the organization, you want to see it protected, so your instincts are going to trend toward defense automatically. However, it is a lot of weight to keep on your shoulders.

As we've said time and again, you are going to have a lot of responsibility in a crisis. If your team is large enough to shoulder other roles, then you can certainly act as Defender and keep the ship afloat. If you also work as a Specialist or Conductor, you might find that your tendency to shift into defense detracts from your ability to do your job.

A Defender can be risk averse, which is not the quality you want in a leader. The heads of organizations *have* to take risks.

If they don't, they tread water until they run out of money. In combat, Mike often had advisors discussing the overall risk of a particular mission. Sometimes that risk simply wasn't worth it, but many times Mike had to make a tough call and send people into harm's way. That's a responsibility of leadership, and the inability to make those decisions can be detrimental.

If you decide not to act as the Defender, you'll likely still take on the role from time to time. Leaders should be protective of their teams, and it's okay to let your compassion for your group overcome your need to take risks. Just remember that you won't reach your end game if you're standing still.

BUILDING THE TEAM BEFORE THE STORM

When should you start building a team for a crisis? To be blunt, right now. The second you finish reading this sentence. Seriously, why are you still reading? Place a bookmark and get to work.

As we've said, a crisis doesn't arrive on your schedule. It appears when you least expect it, often at the worst possible time (thank you, Murphy). If you wait until disaster has struck to start looking for these avatars, it might be too late.

You've already built a great team for your organization. You've made tough decisions in hiring and training personnel to accomplish a variety of tasks. It's likely that you noticed these traits already. In fact, as you were reading this chapter, we bet you recognized some aspects of your own people. Now you need to discuss this with them.

Your team needs to understand your intent throughout the crisis. That provides their guardrails; even absent your direct guidance, they'll be less likely to deviate from the real mission. Most importantly, your team needs to function. They need to work together and watch out for each other, managing stress just as they manage the crisis.

Don't assume that you know everything about an employee, no matter how well you know them. A crisis is a baptism by fire, and nobody can predict how they'll respond to a disaster. Are they the type of person to run toward the chaos or run away? Plenty of people talk big, but fewer are prepared for the actual action.

We recommend you call a meeting and discuss a potential crisis. There are plenty of examples to choose from. Ask them which avatar they identify with the most. Make note of which roles you feel they could fill and which roles you don't have yet. Depending on your organization, you might not have a Maverick or a Diplomat. That doesn't mean you need to hire someone right away, it just means you have a gap that will need to be filled in the future.

Identify the strengths and weaknesses on your team before they are tested at their limits. The reason so many organizations fail in a crisis isn't because they are bad people or lazy. It comes down to one of the most important factors—from a military standpoint—of a successful mission: surprise. When we are surprised, we are going to revert to whatever training or instinct feels right. If you fail to prepare for a crisis, you are preparing to fail a crisis.

This is why the military conducts drills, both planned and unplanned, to test tactics and leadership and staff. When the chaos begins, there won't be time to stop and catch your breath and ask for directions. In that 911 moment, in that golden hour, seconds matter. If you spend even just an hour a month thinking through scenarios and discussing roles, you are light-years ahead of so many others.

And if you identify possible end games based on these scenarios, your first choices can already be made to position you for the future. When that first phase begins, you'll know what to do.

The task force in Pakistan prevented a disaster from becoming a catastrophe. They saved hundreds of thousands of lives and prevented additional destruction from follow-on effects. While the world watched, Mike and his team pulled off a resounding victory. It was a picture-perfect example of how the world can work together for the betterment of humanity. Pakistan was truly grateful for the support. It was a genuine moment of positive change for the region.

With so many groups working together to achieve a larger goal, Mike found a key that determines the success or failure of any crisis: communication.

CHAPTER 4

SET
COMMUNICATION

SECURITY, AS A BUSINESS, IS DRIVEN BY REPUTATION
and networks. It's an industry that requires trust and connections, and there are few ways to gain trust faster than sitting
down face-to-face for an honest discussion. In early 2020,
business at Concentric moved along at a confident and steady
pace. Mike and Roderick each brought their own perspectives to building relationships with clients and securing new
revenue streams.

Mike introduced the concept of virtual conferencing when
he had arrived, but it was seen as a fail-safe rather than a
primary means of communication. Once a client purchased
a service, they could expect to see someone from Concentric

at least once a month—and possibly more—depending on the level of services needed. This approach helped the company to stand out from the competition, as it was seen as not only highly competent and practical, but personable as well. Its Seattle and San Francisco offices were always open—a place for clients to pop in and say hello. Concentric staff is always welcoming, friendly, and open to answering questions that a prospective client might have. Mike and Roderick traveled around the globe to share their ideas and convince new customers to join their team.

In February 2020, Mike and Roderick held a conference with approximately sixty potential clients. It was business as usual as they worked the room. In March of 2020, the first identified case of COVID-19 arrived a mere three miles from the Concentric Seattle office.

As scientists and immunologists determined the severity of the outbreak, the Centers for Disease Control and Prevention (CDC) and World Health Organization (WHO) declared a pandemic. Governments enacted strict quarantine and lockdown procedures to combat this once-in-a-century threat. Suddenly, international travel—or in-person meetings of any kind—were off the table.

Concentric, along with tens of thousands of other businesses around the country, faced a devastating crisis. It wasn't just losing the ability to talk face-to-face with clients. It meant no in-person visits to distant sites, no international travel—curtailing 40 percent of their revenue stream—and a distinct change to the quality of their service.

Mike and Roderick knew that without international clients they needed to make up nearly half of their revenue. This meant refocusing on domestic companies and cyber threats. However, the first problem wasn't finding new clients; it was ensuring their current roster knew they were still operational. Quite simply, they needed to communicate to the world that they were still open for business.

They quickly opened up lines of communication to announce their continued support for the employees and clients of Concentric. The message was short and to the point: For the people of Concentric, know that you are still employed and supported. For clients, both existing and future, we are here and we have your back with whatever security needs this pandemic may bring.

In the absence of communication, people tend to assume the worst. While disasters could take down power lines and affect cell towers and radio signals, most breakdowns in communication are caused by user error: Someone had the information, but they failed to share it. They didn't know where to go to get correct information. Or they were just so overwhelmed that they completely shut down.

Communication comes in many different forms and with many different uses, but it is a critical function of crisis management. It is how you keep your team focused on the end game. It's how to assure the people in your circle that you are still in business and ready to work. It's how you connect with clients and vendors and support. If you are unable to communicate—plainly put—you will fail.

BOTTOM LINE UP FRONT (BLUF, FOR THOSE FAMILIAR): COMMUNICATION IS EVERYTHING

Communication is about relationships: building, strengthening, and reaffirming relationships—the lifeblood of your business. In its purest form, communication is the exchange of information between two or more parties. If you have something to say and can express that to someone else, you are communicating. If you cannot properly communicate, those relationships will wither and your business will dry out. During a crisis especially, a breakdown in communication will be the critical point of failure.

In a crisis, your communication methodology needs to be more focused and effective. This isn't the time to try out new channels or hubs, as the people in your network won't know where to find those. If you have a clear end game, you should know when to use mass communication, more personal missives, or tactical intelligence briefs. Keep things simple and break down your messaging to this:

- WHO needs to know this

- WHAT do they need to know

- WHEN do they need to know this by

- WHERE can they find more information

- WHY is this important right now

A key to solid communications is to always place the bottom line up front—or, in military parlance, the BLUF. No matter what you are saying, or how you are saying it, get the important part of the message out early. Whether it's in an email, letter, or mailer, this means literally putting the key information in the first lines—hence Bottom Line Up Front.

In a crisis, communication is about collecting and disseminating information, but it is also a key tool in building relationships, providing mental health support, and gathering intelligence. Depending on your business, communication might be a tool for driving revenue. Most importantly, as leaders, you need to have clear communication up and down the chain. You need to know the full scope of your crisis.

There are countless tools available in this Age of Information. With such a broad subject, it is easy to be overwhelmed. That's why we concentrate all of our communication through a simple filter. Is your communication strategic or tactical?

STRATEGIC COMMUNICATION

Strategic communication is about the big picture. You are afforded countless tools to express your message, both internally and externally. However, this isn't a one-size-fits-all situation. If you're not using the right tools for the job, you could be wasting money, time, or another valuable resource. Therefore, strategic communication should also be short: this is the length of an elevator pitch, and it should take thirty seconds or less.

It's important to think about both the external and internal communication strategy as you enter a crisis. What message are you using to connect with your clients, and what are you saying to the rest of your team? For Concentric, the external message was "we are open"; the internal message was "we have your back, and we are going to move forward as a company." And your strategy should be reflected across all methods of communication.

As a leader, you are responsible for managing the big picture. If *you* aren't thinking about the end game of your crisis, nobody is. Your strategic communication is about your end game. In that sense, everything you're saying is meant to move you closer to that final goal.

Strategic communication is also about psychology, about affecting the recipient's perception in some way. In Pakistan, the sound of rescue helicopters—the "Angels of Mercy" as the locals referred to them—represented a form of strategic communication. It announced that help was here and available. Often, after a few flybys over the most remote areas, survivors would place stone SOS notices on the ground, enabling their rescue.

Think about the commercials you saw during the height of COVID-19. Many were informative, teaching the basics of handwashing and mask-wearing. As the phases moved on, they became tools to reinvigorate the population after months of lockdown and uncertainty. This message pivoted because, for the government, the end game was a population that felt secure in returning to normal life.

Finally, it is critical to understand that communication doesn't happen in a void. Knowing your audience is a critical part of effective communication. Fortunately, you should have found a Diplomat within your organization for this very purpose.

Once you know the "what" of your overall message, it's time to decide the "how."

TACTICAL COMMUNICATION

As we said earlier, strategic communication is short and sweet, a thirty-second pitch: "We're here to help," "Concentric is open for business," "Snickers satisfies." It is the mission, summarized for a global audience. Tactical communication, on the other hand, is about objectives that take you toward your end game. These are practical and actionable goals.

Tactical communication is the "how" of your strategy. How often are you going to send out this message? Through which means and channels will this message be delivered? How can you deploy A/B testing to refine your message into its most effective form? Your tactical approach supports your strategic goals.

At Concentric, we found that there was a holy trinity of communication right at our fingertips: email, phone calls, and text messages. These are familiar methods to clients, are cost-effective, and could quickly be adjusted as we tested new messaging.

In modern business, email is king. It is the modern-day missive, and a well-designed email is far more effective at strategic communication than even an energetic phone call. In Pakistan, Mike set up call centers run by locals where people were able to call in to request support, ask questions, and get the help they needed. This also allowed him to collate the data on these calls and learn more about the needs of different regions. Finally, text messages are low-cost mailers, with the added benefit of hyperlinks to instantly connect the receiver to your website or any number of other sites. They have the benefit of arriving in your customers' pockets.

Tactical communication with the team is more urgent and direct, and provides guidance during the crisis. This type of communication should be used sparingly to avoid micromanaging. Remember, your job is to lead and focus on the end game. Provide guidance on where you need your team to be, and trust they'll find a way to get there.

BE THE JUNCTION BOX

Effective communication isn't a one-way street. In fact, you can't expect to succeed in a crisis if you don't consume as much information as you put out. That's why we think it's important to develop a clear communication plan for your company: Be the Junction Box.

A junction box, if you're unfamiliar, is where lines of communication converge. In this case, employees are acting as the filter for information moving up and down the chain. There are going to be things you learn in a crisis that need to be understood by the entire team, but there is also a lot of chaff and pointless information spread around. It is important for you to see and understand the big picture and for the team to focus on their lanes.

Vice Admiral Mike LeFever presenting at the Pentagon Public Affairs Press Corps in 2010.

Being the center of information also allows you to sort raw data before it spreads. After the 2008 elections in Pakistan, the Taliban decided to make a statement with VBIEDs (vehicle-borne improvised explosive devices). They had intended to blow up the Parliament building, but instead detonated outside of a Marriott Hotel. It was a tragic event, and a number of people lost their lives. It was a new crisis in the midst of an ongoing one, and—as such—misinformation quickly spread.

During a crisis, competing stories *will* come out of different
organizations. Someone needs to interpret the data and look
for discrepancies (and similarities) in the reports. The US
Ambassador in Pakistan worked with Mike to source accurate information and develop a single message regarding
the attack. It was one story sent to fifty-five different email
addresses, ensuring the right people knew what had really
happened—or at the very least understood as much as those
on the ground.

*Admiral LeFever, Ambassador Croker, and COL Lugo showing
Secretary of Defense Donald Rumsfeld MASH 212 in Muzaffarabad, Pakistan on December 21, 2005.*

Top-down dissemination is important, but so is bottom-up
dissemination. Your "boots on the ground" employees know
the situation better than most. Your front line is incredibly

valuable in helping you, as the leader, to understand the impact of decisions so that you can course correct or take advantage quickly. As you gain new information from subordinates, you have to decide which knowledge is important to spread around. Sometimes information is confidential or could potentially damage you if it got to your competition.

Finally, sharing information helps strengthen relationships. Internally, your employees will feel ownership of the business if you include them on the inside. Your clients will appreciate your transparency.

COMMAND AND CONTROL

Communication is an effective way to express command and control within your company. You need to establish guidelines for your employees and reinforce that often. By setting up a culture where information flows in the correct manner, you won't have to fight to get something from your people. It also means you won't be blindsided when your PR team makes an announcement that wasn't ready to go out.

At Concentric, we held weekly meetings with leaders and our PR team to discuss the goals during the crisis, which included communication. We talked about the messages that we wanted to go out and the platforms that we wanted to use. Rather than micromanage the teams, we set the expectations for tasks to complete and goals to meet week to week. If there was an issue, we could address it at the next meeting to course correct.

These meetings served a number of purposes:

- We could state clearly our objectives and expectations so there was no confusion about what we wanted said both internally and externally.

- We were able to get feedback from our leaders so we knew if we were still on track for our end game.

- Most importantly, we were able to set goals and deadlines that kept us on track.

Depending on the size of your company, your subordinate leaders should be doing the same thing. They act as junction boxes within their departments. They hold meetings and set deadlines and milestones. By communicating clearly and explaining your path forward as a team, you empower them to make decisions that move you forward through the crisis.

Finally, an effective way to control communication is through your company website. If set up properly, the site includes contact information that guides outside sources to the correct people. You can use access points to filter out customers and employees from regular people. This is a more high-tech and streamlined version of a phone tree, and more pleasant for the user overall.

MAKE THE RIGHT CALLS

Communication is all about relationships and the flow of information. In a crisis, you can't work toward your end game if you don't actually know where you are. You have to build and maintain a trusted network both above and below. You need to build a culture of open communication within your team and test your network to plug any leaks.

- In all communication, put the Bottom Line Up Front

- Strategic communication is about your big picture

- Tactical communication is about how you will operate

- Be the Junction Box and disseminate information to your team

- Remember that communication is key to leading your company

A UNITED MESSAGE

As Concentric expanded our focus following the lockdowns, we reached out to our network to let them know that the doors were open and we were still in business. We stood on the precipice of a potential fall that could bankrupt the company. Fortunately for us, we had chosen our path correctly and connected to the right network.

We were able to define our market through careful use of mass media and a redesign of the site to cater to new clientele. While we had once acted as generalists in the security field, now we had a focused business track that clearly connected to the new way of doing business during COVID-19.

We increased our business. New clients arrived so fast that we could barely keep up. Even better, we were able to keep our entire team employed and cared for throughout the crisis. Clear communication ensured that customers understood what we could do for them, and our staff understood what we *needed* from them and that we would take care of them.

During a crisis, people are quick to assume the worst. You have the ability to reassure them that you have a path forward. If you have a clear message and use the right tools to deliver it, know that you will be heard.

CHAPTER 5

INTELLIGENCE

Only moments after landing in Pakistan for the first time, Mike was back in the air. He'd read the briefings and listened to reports from those already on the ground following the earthquake. However, a crisis breeds rumors and misinformation. The first thing Mike needed was a good, old-fashioned recon mission for his own "eyes on."

In the military, intelligence is a catch-all term that means sourced and assessed information. Teams gather intelligence from a variety of locations and spend hours connecting dots and removing unnecessary details. Leaders at the top need condensed, clear briefings that allow them to make key decisions as fast as possible. As General George S. Patton said, "A good plan...executed now is better than the perfect plan executed next week."

Admiral LeFever, conducting a surveillance of the affected region, embarked on TF Griffin Chinook.

Mike brought along an experienced intelligence officer on his mission to Pakistan. While the situation was different than they had perhaps trained for, gathering information wasn't all that dissimilar than from a warzone. They needed to analyze trends, make contacts on the ground and build a HUMINT network (human intelligence, or intelligence gathered through interpersonal contact), and establish CCIRs (Commander Critical Information Requirements).

A crisis moves very quickly, so a sense of urgency was necessary. Mike pushed his teams to prioritize fact-finding. They also needed to set up procedures to push new intel toward the top so Mike would be able to make accurate and timely decisions. It wouldn't do to make a call that was hours behind the curve.

The team held daily briefings, and afterward the intelligence officer and their team poured over all the information collected to find patterns and potential points of friction. Data mining in the field is like assembling a puzzle with all the pieces turned facedown. You can't really say what the final image will be until you've gathered the information—and you're almost never operating with a complete picture. This is why a good intel team knows how to extrapolate from a few pieces of data.

Mike relied on his intel team to determine where potential follow-on crises may appear. This enabled him to see the big picture clearer. When determining his end game and planning his path toward it, this information protected him and the team from running into serious problems. Moreover, having confidence in the macro of the crisis enabled Mike to make decisions faster.

Leaders in a crisis need to have that same mentality, especially in the early phases when decisions can literally mean life or death. Situations evolve rapidly, and they deteriorate just as fast. Gathering information, and determining its value, must be a priority.

Now as an old Marine captain once said, "Words mean stuff." Since we have a few terms in this chapter that are often conflated, let's establish our definitions:

- **Data** is raw facts gathered from multiple sources

- **Information** is cohesive presentation of a sequence of events or things

- **Intelligence** is a refined and vetted collection of information

- **Misinformation** is unintentionally incorrect information

- **Disinformation** is intentionally incorrect information

YOU DON'T KNOW
WHAT YOU DON'T KNOW

Admiral Eric Olson often said, "When the map differs from the terrain, go with the terrain."

One of the biggest causes of indecision during a crisis is uncertainty. Without a clear picture of the world around you, it is easy to fall into fight or flight. The problem is that a crisis doesn't wait around for you to be ready. It is an ever-changing operating picture. More often than not, what you think you know is already wrong. That's why you need to prioritize intelligence gathering in your team.

No matter how you gather information—with a dedicated team, with internet research, hiring a consulting firm—it is vital that you vet and cross-reference what you find. Intel requires constant reassessment and revalidation, which makes reviewing your data and listening to actual experts critical if you're exploring a more technical field.

As with many aspects of your crisis management, you'll be working with limited resources. That means that it is your responsibility to focus your time, energy, and money in the right direction. You'll quickly learn which sources provide actionable information and which are just sharing gossip.

However, none of this is of any use if you don't apply it to an action.

INFORMATION THAT LEADS TO ACTION

Intelligence is sourced and vetted information that leads to action. While this isn't the military definition, it is how we've operated at Concentric during crises and normal business hours. If you're not doing anything with the intel at your disposal, then why did you collect it in the first place?

You will have a fire hose of information aimed at you during a crisis. As a leader, you need to set up a synthesizer within your organization. While you are the junction box for communication, you will need help sorting through raw data. Your role is to make key decisions, which means you'll need refined intel. It's important to establish what we would call Commander's Critical Information Requirement or CCIRs.

In the military, a CCIR is a criteria for pushing intel to the top. If a Soldier bumps their knee and has to sit out a training event, that's probably not important to the General commanding the base. However, if a platoon of infantry is lost in the field and needs a rescue, the base commander needs to know.

Good intel connects dots and reveals patterns. For Concentric, we needed to know about growing trends in the market. We saw that tech companies were better prepared to weather lockdowns and quarantines than other industries. We also saw how many businesses needed to quickly pivot to an online marketplace. This not only helped us understand how we could protect our own organization, but where new niches were forming that we could fill.

In Pakistan, Mike needed information to help him decide how best to deploy his resources and direct food, medical, and other relief supplies where they were needed. He didn't always have leaders from the community approaching with a clear list of their needs. Some NGOs (non government organizations) and refugees were skeptical about working with Americans, especially the US military; some were too proud to admit that they needed help. On the ground, the humanitarian teams, the Pakistan Military units, and US helicopter crews deployed to the affected regions gathered raw data about which distribution points were running out before others, or where the most tents had been deployed. While these data points didn't add up to much themselves, the intel officer was able to see a pattern develop. Certain areas of the country had been hit harder, yet needed fewer assets. They were more self-sufficient and established their own networks for supplies. With that knowledge, Mike was able to redirect food and medical support to areas that needed it most.

Evaluating these signs and determining the accurate meaning is a skill, and you might not have it. Intel officers train for years to comb through data points in search of actionable information. In the same way, there are consulting companies that have done the work to understand what certain patterns mean for your business. Depending on your situation, you need to bring in the right experts to help you fill in your knowledge gaps.

These experts help you separate valid information from hearsay. Try to be specific with your goals and needs as you put these teams together. If they don't know what you want to learn, you might end up with a pile of information that you can't really use or that perhaps doesn't do anything to help you find your end game.

Useful information affords you clarity. If you learn something from your team and it hasn't helped you understand the big picture or make an important decision, then it wasn't something you needed to know at that moment.

MAKING A SMOOTH DECISION

Under normal circumstances, your team has a standard operational speed. In a given week, you will accomplish a certain number of tasks. You'll make this many calls to that many clients and grow your business a small amount. In a crisis, people start to move faster, and that brings mistakes.

Burn this into your mind: Slow is smooth, and smooth is fast. Don't rush just because you feel a sense of urgency. Prioritize, but take on challenges at a steady and controlled pace. That includes how you digest and take action on intelligence.

However, you need to balance patience with the reality of your ticking clock. The time you think you have...you don't have. While it would be great to wait for all of the cards to be dealt before making a choice, you will more often need to make decisions without all of the intelligence. Surviving and thriving in a crisis means acting with the best information available. And remember, no decision is *still* a decision.

A crisis often feels dire, no matter the actual stakes of the situation. You might be worried about making the wrong move, so you try to slow down too much. It's a common mistake, and it comes from a lack of confidence or a lack of experience. Intelligence helps you see beyond the short term, so you can make a choice and move forward. You can also use this information to build contingencies that offer you multiple paths to follow. That way, when you need to make a quick decision, you already have a direction to go.

SOURCES OF INFORMATION

A key aspect of intelligence gathering is knowing your sources. From primary and secondary to nontraditional entities, there is a glut of information to be gathered. The more sources available, the more likely you'll be able to find an accurate bit of intelligence.

Gathering information in a crisis might seem alien if you've never done it before, but it won't be as difficult as you might think. People want to share what they've heard during a crisis. Think about any time you've been at the office when there is a major news story. "Did you see this?" "Did you hear that?" "My brother's friend's cousin says this!"

Primary sources of information are firsthand accounts. These can be eyewitness statements, documents from a business, images from a satellite, and so on. Primary sources don't often come with all the context, but they are—more often than not—accurate in their depiction. In most cases, be cautious since first reports are not always the most accurate.

Secondary sources can be reports and analyses. While these provide context, they might also include bias. If you read a write-up of a political candidate written by the opposition, they might include some spin that leans the article more toward their point of view. With secondary sources, you'll need to interpret the data with this intended (or unintended) bias in mind.

Tertiary sources usually include encyclopedias or larger reports, in which the secondary sources are again reviewed and summarized. Important details might be left out, leading these analyses to be less useful in the long run.

Finally, you have a plethora of nontraditional sources for information. In our modern age, technology has made intel gathering even easier. So long as the crisis leaves the Internet intact, you'll have the world at your fingertips. Social media is a gathering point for all manner of data, although you should approach it with caution. Just as information has grown more available, misinformation has become far more abundant. It's very easy to be swept up by a lie before you've even scratched the surface of the truth.

Most of the intel you're gathering isn't some big secret. You're not trying to find out what's happening in Area 51; you're trying to learn the reality of your crisis. Most experts want the truth to spread, so everyone is properly informed. Insiders want to share, so it makes them appear more knowledgeable. Even your competitors will put out information to build confidence in their customers. You won't hurt for sources; you'll just have to do the work refining that raw data into something useful.

Once you have intel, you have to decide how to disseminate it. Of course, members of your team need to know, but what about clients? What about superiors? What about the competition?

TALKING TO THE COMPETITION

Outside of a crisis, you have your alliances drawn up with fairly strong borders. Certain companies or people are allies, others are neutral, and some are direct competitors. Competition is a part of running any business, and it can be a healthy way to keep your team motivated.

In a crisis, however, the rules change.

A crisis builds bridges where they couldn't exist before. Your fiercest rival might be going through the same crisis as you, and that offers opportunities. By sharing information, you help ensure the longevity of your industry. Their success can bolster your success—a rising tide raises all vessels. You might even build up the relationship to the point that you're no longer competitive but rather become cooperative.

Not to say there aren't risks. Concentric chose to be transparent with some of our competitors. It backfired only once: there was a company—that shall remain nameless—that chose to violate our trust to undermine our credibility with clients. It didn't have the desired effect, and most of our competitors were grateful for the help and chose to share their information as well. Some of those relationships grew pretty strong, even after we left the most dire parts of the crisis.

Mike saw similar opportunities in Pakistan. A recovery effort of this size isn't possible unless multiple nations come together. The US has the ability to bring support rapidly, but resources run dry quickly. That's why so many other countries needed to lend a hand. For some, it was a global stage to demonstrate goodwill.

Iran and China along with the rest of the world sent planes filled with supplies. When the news organizations saw the Chinese and Iranian flags flying next to the stars and stripes, with citizens from around the world working together, it created a powerful moment. It was a "softball pitch" that Mike was happy to hit.

Mike was often asked, "How are you getting along with members of these nations when politically things are so tense?" It was easy to answer: "This situation isn't about politics, it's about people coming together to help one another and save lives." Everyone gets to come out of the situation looking better. While it may not be the masterstroke that builds alliances on a geopolitical scale, it certainly helped improve public standing for the nations involved.

UNDERSTANDING A WORLD TURNED UPSIDE DOWN

Intelligence is a cure for uncertainty, and that's not just about you as a leader. Each department, each individual needs to have a clear idea of what is happening and what they need to do next. Intelligence allows you to build a common operating picture. Once your team has an accurate perspective of the crisis, they are able to function at a higher level.

- Understand that a crisis is chaos, and you won't always know what you don't know

- Establish a team to intake raw data, refine the information, and vet for actionable intelligence that moves you forward

- Cast a wide net to gather information, even looking to nontraditional indicators

- Evaluate your sources of information constantly

- Share your intel within and outside of your organization

When your crisis begins, follow Mike's lead and hop into that helicopter for early reconnaissance. Gather information and make it a priority for everyone in your organization. Remember that time is never on your side, but fight the urge to rush. You'll have to make decisions with limited information, but constant action will give you a smooth and steady pace.

In the early phases of the crisis, misinformation spreads rapidly. Be wary of accepting intel that fits perfectly in your worldview. Sometimes the truth will hurt, but you can't hope to survive without it.

Intelligence allows you to see the full scope of the world around you. It provides context to the crisis and affords you the confidence to make tough decisions. As you move through the coming challenges, remember to stay flexible and focused on where you want to go.

CHAPTER 6

REFIT

WHEN HE FIRST ARRIVED IN PAKISTAN, MIKE WASN'T sure if he had the right tools for the job. He quickly learned that any tool could work, so long as he focused on his end game.

The modern US military is a modular force, combining units in order to approach any specific mission. Engineers and infantry team up with ordnance and transportation, pocketing small units of intelligence and civil affairs as well. It's a chimera trained for a singular purpose, allowing battalions and brigades to adapt, but only so far. Mike had trained for a mission in Iraq and around the theater, and his team was built and supplied for that same objective. Now, he had to take his square peg and fit it into a round hole.

One of the first challenges was establishing potable water stations and medical centers, but luckily the ESG came ready with that ability. Combat operations required hydration as well, so combined units always had the ability to treat and maintain water sources. The MASH was designed to provide combat field trauma and intensive care support, so it could quickly convert to manage a mass casualty event.

The second challenge was food. Pakistan is a predominately Muslim country, and the majority only consume halal food, a religious standard of meal preparation. They would not eat just anything that the team prepared. Until a proper mess could be established, Mike needed to provide the tens of thousands of refugees with acceptable meals. Fortunately, he didn't have to look far. As the US military is a multidenominational group, special meals are provided for Muslim service members. Mike was able to call up his stores of halal MREs. This acted as a stopgap until proper facilities were erected.

US Naval Mobile Seabee Construction Battalion (NMCB) 4 and 74 assisting local Pakistanis in removal of rubble from the earthquake devastation.

Finally, Mike looked at his assembled vehicles as untapped platforms of possibility. By removing a few seats from a Humvee, they created a makeshift ambulance. By clearing equipment from their helicopters, they suddenly had heavy lift and rapid-response medical transport. One by one, he went through the resources available and repurposed them to meet the needs of the crisis.

TF Eagle unloading Australian TF 632 personnel and equipment at Dhanni, Pakistan. The roads in the Neelum Valley were so severely damaged that the only way TF 632 could establish a camp was to be flown in by helicopters.

From every angle, Mike found new problems to solve. He had assembled his team for the theater, so his interpreters spoke fluent Arabic or Kurdish. In Pakistan, however, the primary languages are Urdu, Pashto, and Sindhi, and there are nearly a dozen others throughout the various regions. Iraq's terrain was mostly level with some highlands in the north, while Pakistan had mountainous regions with some nearly unreachable without a helicopter. Mike and his team had to rethink how they used their equipment. They had to reimagine everything they knew about their gear, their supplies, and their combat methodology in order to face the current crisis.

In short, they needed to innovate.

While there are many tenets of crisis management that come and go through the phases, innovation is a constant—and it is the same for businesses adapting to crisis requirements.

WHAT YOU HAVE IS WHAT YOU NEED

A refit is retooling what you already have for new uses. Whether hardware, processes, or even people, a refit allows you to tackle a crisis from a different angle. As new challenges arise during a crisis, you don't have the luxury of time and resources to explore solutions. Often, you have to make do with what you have nearby. Most companies don't have endless capital to throw at problems or buy something new.

How you approach a refit depends on your situation and your end game. The solutions that work for a service company won't be the same as for a security company. You need confidence in your abilities and in your team. When you make a decision to move in a new direction, or to try something out of the ordinary, you have to commit fully. There is a great military expression for innovation: "If it was stupid and it works, it wasn't stupid."

Stop looking for what you want, and start recognizing what you need. Instead of asking for a Jeep Grand Cherokee, say you need a vehicle that can carry a specific load. This change in outlook focuses on the requirements of the task rather than the item you once had in mind. The more a company and team can repurpose and turbo-charge the familiar, the higher the degree of organizational and team unity in forging the way forward.

At the height of the worst COVID-19 surges, hospitals ran out of ICU beds. Instead of asking specifically for more intensive care facilities, they looked internally at what resources already existed in the building. Operating rooms, hallways, even closets were converted into functioning facilities for struggling patients. When personnel shortages threatened their ability to manage the caseload, hospitals instituted buddy systems to train up newer staff on ICU procedures.

A refit takes the resources on hand and looks at them from a practical standpoint. "What else can these do?" Whether that's a piece of equipment, an employee, or a building, evoking a culture of innovation opens up possibilities that allow you to meet your needs without adding anything new.

Keep an open mind and an active imagination. A crisis isn't a time to think restrictively. Sometimes you need an outside-the-box idea to fix a seemingly impossible problem.

Part of your job as a leader is defining innovation for your team. What solutions do you want to find? What areas of your business are open to experimentation? Could some new idea get you to your end game sooner? Introduce these questions to key leaders and ask them to return with concepts. Tell them that there are no wrong answers.

This is also a great excuse to bring in newer team members and let them loose on a problem. Sometimes experience can hamper creativity. You "know" what works and what doesn't work, so you're less likely to try something truly radical. Someone new to the industry might have a path to success well off the beaten trail.

Once you've introduced a culture of experimentation, you open the doors to inventive solutions. You won't need to fear challenges because you'll have a team of people focused on developing creative solutions.

Finally, conduct "vector checks" to make sure your refit meets your needs. Once the idea becomes too risky or too wasteful, it's time to rein in your creativity.

DON'T WAIT FOR A CRISIS

Don't wait for a crisis to start planning. Look at your tools and experiment with how they can tackle other tasks. You can take more risks when the consequences of failure aren't so dire. Most importantly, you can build that mentality and culture in your organization.

In a crisis, you're not often faced with the impossible. Usually, the challenges that arise were coming anyway, and the crisis just hastened their arrival. Whatever your timeline might have been, be prepared to bump it up. If you're not thinking about innovation already, now is the time to start. You can't plan for everything, but you will feel more prepared with options in your back pocket.

This doesn't mean that you should sit down and try to think up every possible scenario. Instead, take stock of what tools, processes, and personnel you have at your disposal. What are the inherent traits already organic to your company? Even if you don't know what the future holds, you'll feel more confident by knowing your true capabilities.

NECESSITY IS THE MOTHER OF INVENTION

We consulted with a small business some years ago shortly after they experienced a crisis. Our services focused on security, but we were interested about the lessons they had learned along the way. The manager couldn't wait to share his story.

They had been in a steady state for years, operating but never thriving. It wasn't a problem with the staff; they worked hard and got the job done. It wasn't a problem with branding; people that needed their services knew who they were and where to find them. Still, the business was stagnant. Then came a crisis.

The manager knew that staying the course would mean the end of the business. They had to come up with a solution fast, and leadership didn't have one. After briefing the entire team on the situation, they grouped together to brainstorm courses of action. Suddenly, the lights came on for the staff. Ideas flew around the room in a flurry, often leading nowhere but sometimes bringing a spark of potential. By the end of the day, they had several workable answers to their current crisis.

Even better, they had come up with new ideas and innovations for their existing problems. As the crisis came to a close, the manager saw his business positioned even better than before. He jokingly told us that he wished he could create a crisis every day. We reminded him that his employees didn't just respond to the event, but rather that they were entrusted with finding solutions. It provided ownership in the business and a culture of respect.

These brainstorming sessions are a great way to discover new traits within your organization, but you'll need to test out ideas to see if they actually hold water. Experimentation is a crucial part of the process. You won't know if something works until you actually put it into practice. If it fails, that's just another lesson to learn.

EXPERIMENTATION, ERRORS, AND EVOLUTION

In a crisis, you might be afraid to experiment since the stakes are so high. However, this is the moment when you *need* to innovate. There are going to be missteps along the way toward your end game, and some may be rather large.

Roderick often jokes that "Failing is bad. You shouldn't do it." However, trial and error is a stepping stone to success. If you're not failing, you're not trying.

During normal times, we tend to be risk averse. Why take a chance if it could cost us time, resources, or money? You can't focus on the potential for failure or you won't try at all. Instead, approach each experiment with the idea that you'll learn a valuable lesson. Instill confidence in your team to try.

Let your team know early on that experimentation is encouraged. You want to try out their ideas and record the results. Be scientific in your approach; just because something worked one time doesn't necessarily mean it will *always* work. In the same vein, just because it *didn't* work one time doesn't mean you should discount it completely.

You can go a step further and *prepare* for failure. This doesn't mean you should *anticipate* failure, but rather build a safety net in case it falls through. During the 2011 raid on Usama bin Laden's compound, the SEALs arrived in two helicopters. They knew the risks of the mission, including the possibility of a loss of an air asset. Hovering over the yard to off-load troops, the helicopter's tail boom clipped the wall, bringing it down hard. Fortunately, the SEALs had planned for the loss of one transport and were able to complete their mission and exfiltrate on the backup chopper.

As a leader, you need to understand, evaluate, and mitigate risk. Every decision you make has some level of risk attached, and it's no different when trying a radical approach to solve a problem in the midst of a crisis. You have to decide how much risk you can accept if the idea turns out to be wrong.

Prepare for potential consequences, but be proactive. Before you start experimenting, discuss with your team the worst-case scenarios, so you can design and implement mitigation measures. Let your teams know that there is no shame in failure, just that they need to learn lessons from each attempt so they can grow closer to a real solution.

APPLYING INNOVATION

As you evaluate the assets already in your possession, don't focus on specific crises to come. You can't prepare for everything, and you won't always see what's about to strike. Instead, build internal confidence in the tools you have and the people you've trained.

- Look at what you already have before you consider finding or buying something from outside. It's easier to supercharge a familiar tool than learn something new.

- Don't wait for a crisis to take stock in your assets, processes, and people.

- Necessity drives invention, but you can discover these opportunities outside of a crisis as well.

- Don't be afraid to fail, although certainly don't plan
to either.

Mike was able to convert combat gear and vehicles for a
humanitarian mission. Attack helicopters and troop trans-
ports became makeshift ambulances, and his combat forces
dove into the chaos to clear debris and save lives. While the
disaster in Pakistan was far from over, the innovative thinking
of the assembled team had proven its worth.

For the next few months, Mike continued to build on his
successes and reinforce the culture of experimentation within
his subordinate leaders. Hospitals popped up around the country, followed by growing refugee cities, schools, and places of
work. He knew that the path to success required a bit of risk,
but the reward would be great. All told, hundreds of thousands
of lives were saved and improved by the coalition.

Mike and Roderick often look at the risks they've taken over
the years and review the outcomes. Now, with Concentric,
they are confident in their ability to adapt. They don't fear any
coming crisis because they know how they'll respond.

Once you understand the anatomy of a crisis, you'll share that
same confidence.

PHOTO GALLERY

Chartered Ukrainian Antonov AN-225 filled with food supplies in Islamabad, Pakistan. US Air Force 818th Contingency Response Group (CRG) helped offload the supplies for dissemination by Army Chinook CH-47 helicopters from Task Force Griffin.

NMCB 4 and 74 worked to rebuild shelters quickly for families, as winter was fast approaching.

Admiral LeFever sharing US traditions and holidays such as Santa Claus and gift giving with affected Pakistani children.

The helicopters would deliver supplies from Islamabad to the devastated regions and then return with injured personnel.

Everyday life in a refugee camp.

Pakistani children's lives disrupted by the earthquake.

CHAPTER 7

MENTAL HEALTH

IF YOU HAVEN'T SEEN THE HIMALAYAS IN PERSON, THEY are difficult to describe. Stretching from the eastern tip of Afghanistan all the way through Nepal and India, this massive mountain range looms over its host nations, an earthen sentinel capped in perpetual snowy peaks. As Mike traveled around Pakistan overseeing recovery from the earthquake, the Himalayas were always in view. It was a marvelous thing, that the same tectonic plates that had so recently wreaked havoc on the country had—some forty million years earlier—come together to form such a majestic sight.

Working in such mountainous terrain had many disadvantages. Roadways were narrow, and often unimproved, causing convoys to slow and struggle as they raced to get supplies to various towns and villages. More than a few locations could only be reached by air, and helicopter assets were prized by every department in the recovery operation. With so many people in need, Mike had to set up remote operating stations throughout his stretch of the Himalayas.

The teams operated in different regions in the North-West Frontier Province (now called Khyber Pakhtunkhwa). These bases were in remote regions that were devastated by the earthquake and the teams worked seven days a week nonstop seeing patients. The isolation alone took a toll on the men and women deployed to these areas, but witnessing the daily struggle of a people in desperate need—homes destroyed, mass casualties, dwindling resources—sapped the soul. There's only so long a person can manage that kind of stress.

Mike knew it too. While the military trains its people to operate under extreme conditions, there is a price to pay for the daily assault on the psyche. To help alleviate the stress and provide respite, Mike instituted a standard rotation program, bringing his teams out of the field and back to Islamabad for a hot meal, a comfortable bed, and a hot shower.

It may not seem like much, but this respite from the front lines was a lifesaver. Stress is a cumulative injury, and it often doesn't reveal the extent of the damage until long after you've left the danger. There have been countless studies examining the long-term effects of stress on the human body. Post-traumatic stress disorder isn't just a by-product of combat, but of an overwhelming experience. That can be an assault, a car accident, a sudden financial loss, or the sudden death of a loved one. In essence, any crisis will bring with it endless stressors.

Admiral LeFever meeting with Lt. Col. Jamie Gannon and Maj. Livingston of the Combined Medical Relief Team (CMRT), which included 206 Marines and sailors of the 3rd Marine Expeditionary Force (MEF) from Okinawa, Japan. From November 17, 2005, through February 22, 2006, this CMRT treated 14,468 patients, conducted 73 surgeries, performed 570 lab procedures and 493 X-rays, and issued 12,364 immunizations.

As a leader, you need to consider how stress affects your team. It's not just about maintaining productivity or meeting deadlines. If you succeed and lose those around you, then you haven't succeeded at all. One of the most important tasks you will have through every phase of a crisis is caring for the mental health of your people.

THE SILENT KILLER

During the onset of a crisis, you likely won't pay attention to your own mental well-being, let alone that of those around you. There's no time. The 911 moment is a phase marked by reaction and quick decisions. Adrenaline floods your system, keeping you alert and active despite the overwhelming chaos.

The problem is most people never let off the gas. They try to maintain that same level of energy and inertia into Phases 2 and 3, burning out long before the crisis ends.

In a combat environment, Soldiers must maintain a "ready state" from the moment they hit the ground until the moment they leave the zone. Even inside a base, they can't escape the knowledge that they are in a combat zone, under the threat of attack at any moment.

This is the same type of stress you will endure in a crisis. Your body never has the opportunity to recover.

We saw this at Concentric during the COVID-19 pandemic. As a company, we had our own issues to manage, our own personal crisis. At the same time, we were a part of the global calamity and suffered those same stressors as well. After leaving work, we still had to contend with dwindling supplies at grocery stores and endless tragedy on the news. Moreover, we saw how stress affected those around us.

In a startup or early-stage company, your stress level is always above average. You always have the knowledge that your business is this fragile, impermanent thing that must be protected. Add onto that the fear of losing clients, clawing out of the red, and fending off competition, and you have a growing pile of unmanaged stressors. Over time, they will burn you out.

You need to have a plan for the mental wellness of your team—and for yourself—if you want to survive. This can come in a variety of forms, from professional assistance to wellness checks to mental resilience training. However you choose to tackle the problem, the time to prepare is now and the time to acknowledge is always.

It's important to normalize feeling stressed and to find a healthy way to work out your stress until the crisis ends—individually and as a team. As a leader, you need to learn the signs of stress and start planning your mitigation methods now. There are any number of resources to help everyone understand and manage their stress both at work and at home.

WELLNESS CHECKS

Mental health should not be a taboo subject. The military is by no means the only industry suffering a mental health epidemic, but it stands as a stark example of the failure of leadership to account for resiliency and wellness. Every single day, twenty-two service members take their lives. It is a sobering number. While there are numerous causes of suicide, some of the leading factors are depression, substance abuse, and experiences of extreme stress or trauma.

We don't mean to alarm you, but these are factors you need to keep in mind. In a crisis, no matter how calm it may seem, everyone involved is under extreme stress. Your job as a leader is to monitor your team, and yourself, for signs of anxiety and depression.

One of the simplest methods, and yet highly effective, is a wellness check.

It is checking in with your people, by Zoom or a phone call or, if you're in an office, stopping by someone's desk, all with the singular intent to see how they are doing, to ask about them outside from their performance at work. Are their family members doing okay? Are they concerned about anything? This isn't a checklist to run through, but an actual conversation. This will help you—as the leader—to understand everyone's different tolerance levels for stress, as well as how to calibrate response and support going forward to ensure a healthy workforce in crisis.

Mental resilience can be difficult to track during the first phase of a crisis. Adrenaline and momentum keep most people moving forward through constant reaction. It isn't until they have time to sit and think about what is happening before their mind finally catches up. In this way, extreme stress is like a traumatic injury. Often the victim hardly notices the severity of the damage until they have burned through the initial adrenaline burst.

When you're conducting a wellness check, it shouldn't look or feel like a morale booster. A pizza party for an exhausted staff isn't a wellness assessment. Gifts won't cut it. The most important aspect of a check-in is that your employees feel heard. Let them share their concerns and their grief, and honestly answer. You might not have a solution on hand, but you can demonstrate that you are willing to work with them.

EXPERT SUPPORT

In Pakistan, service members experienced incredible strain on a daily basis. If a Soldier began to withdraw from their friends, give away possessions, or speak openly about hurting themselves, those around them were trained to go for help. Rather, they were trained to *escort* the other Soldier to the proper help.

In the military it is called **ACE**. It is a wellness check designed to prevent self-harm, and it follows a basic—if blunt—formula. First, **Ask** the person directly if they are considering hurting themselves. You're never going to give someone an idea by merely asking. Second, **Care** for the person, remaining calm at their side and actively listening. Finally, **Escort** the person to proper care, never sending them alone.

Now, hopefully you will never see your staff reach this level of stress, but it's important to have the information. We would much rather you know it and never need it than the other way around. For less extreme situations, bringing in expert support can look like a number of different things, outlined next.

A Culture of Caring

A wellness check also can be used more broadly, such as with your entire team. These can be conducted daily or weekly, or whenever you feel they are needed. They should serve as the opening to any meeting, a few minutes outside of "business talk" to honestly share concerns as a team.

One such method is the Red, Yellow, Green check. Employees are asked how they rate their mental well-being on a scale of either green—things are as normal as can be—yellow—feeling stressed, but manageable—or red—the stress is out of hand. As employees offer their answer, ask them to elaborate and share what they are comfortable saying. Make the resources available to all employees, and offer to help connect people with support whenever needed.

In Pakistan, Mike deployed his leadership and his Senior Enlisted Advisor—or Command Master Chief/Command Sergeant Major—along with the chaplain to go visit the outstations and teams and speak and listen to their concerns. At Concentric, he asked his director of HR to lead discussions or bring in medical experts on mental resilience and stress management. As CEO, he actively encouraged (and continues to promote) one-on-one discussions with employees throughout the company in order to better understand their individual stressors.

Through a little trial and error, you and your team will be able to find the most effective method. Involve them in the discussion and come prepared with solutions, which may also include seeking help from the outside.

Webinars

We live in a wonderful modern age where you have access to trained professionals on demand at a moment's notice. A number of mental health professionals now offer webinars that you can schedule for your teams.

One important thing to note is that not all webinars are created equal. Before you spend the time and money, you'll want to do your research and be sure this will work for you.

That said, a virtual lecture might not connect with all employees. Some people require more active learning, which means you'll need to connect with a local expert.

Psychologists

A psychologist who comes to your office and listens to your employees is the most powerful tool for mental health treatment. They bring with them not only experience but the knowledge of how to handle a variety of difficult crises.

Bringing a doctor into your office might not always be feasible, but again you can use technology to allow virtual visits for your team. More importantly, a psychologist can recognize the signs of more troubling issues. A leader showing genuine concern is great, but some members of your team won't open up to an authority figure for fear of repercussions. Having an objective source to speak with allows them the freedom to be honest.

However you approach bringing in resources for your organization, you have to do this from a place of authentic and genuine care.

AUTHENTICITY

During a crisis, your team will turn to you for guidance and support. Roderick often noted that, during one crisis or another, their competition flooded employees with cheap gifts to buy continued loyalty. It rarely worked. Under normal circumstances, an empty gesture might pass without a second thought. In a crisis, a lack of authenticity is as helpful as a Band-Aid on a gunshot wound.

One key concept to remember as you approach your team is honesty. They want to know they are supported, but also tell them that they are needed. If they need time or space, be ready to give it to them, but let them know how their efforts make a difference.

As you connect with your company and provide them the support they need, don't forget to conduct a wellness check on the person at the top.

HEAL THYSELF

We talk about a lot of issues in this book, but this is the biggest lesson of all:

If you don't take care of yourself, you *cannot* take care of anyone else.

In the first few weeks of Pakistan, Mike's schedule was nonstop. He'd wake up at 5:00 a.m., meet with the ambassador, rush to the helicopter to tour the day's activities, grab a cup of coffee, have an afternoon of meetings and debriefs with various organizations and countries, possibly get a bite to eat, and then join video conferences with DC. If he was lucky, he'd grab four hours of sleep and start all over again.

You can survive off adrenaline and caffeine for only so long, however. Mike's productivity dropped, and he noticed that he was not as sharp and focused. Finally, his staff approached him. He'd been so concerned about their well-being and their mental state that he'd never focused any energy on himself. Fortunately, he had a great support network there with him.

During the early months of the COVID-19 crisis at Concentric, we checked in on each other regularly. We both worked tirelessly to maintain our business and support our teams, but we were susceptible to the same stress as anyone else. Though we didn't name these unofficial wellness checks, we'd listen to each other for new behaviors or patterns. More importantly, we immediately addressed our concerns.

Self-care is a challenge for leaders. You might not want to show weakness in front of your team or your family, but mental health isn't weakness. There is no shame in needing help, nor in asking for it. You are still the same strong person you were before, only you're taking-better care of your mental well-being. If anything, that makes you a better leader.

As a leader, the health and safety of your team has to be a top priority. Remember:

- You need to learn about and watch for signs of stress during a crisis

- Conduct wellness checks on your team and yourself

- Learn about the resources available in your area, and make sure team members know they can be brought in at any time

- You have to take care of yourself, so that you can take care of others

AWAY FROM THE FRONT LINES

Mike made mental resilience a priority during his time in Pakistan. With thousands of service members, civilians, and organizations from around the world, he had all the support he needed to accomplish the mission and achieve his end game. However, he wouldn't have been successful without taking into account the stress of the crisis.

Those on the front lines faced sensory overload, along with witnessing seemingly endless human suffering. No matter how "tough" someone claims to be, those images and smells and sounds chip away until they expose a raw nerve.

Every crisis will bring new stressors, and the severity of the crisis has little to do with the overall effect on mental health. You have to monitor these effects on your own organization. While you might not be able to eliminate the causes, you can at least mitigate the fallout. Understand that stress is a cumulative disease, and the longer you wait to manage it, the worse the damage will be.

Mental health isn't just about *surviving* a crisis. It's about what happens when the crisis ends. As you connect with your team on a more personal level, you'll notice performance improve throughout the organization. In fact, you might discover that building relationships is one of the most important jobs you'll have in a crisis.

CHAPTER 8

RELATIONSHIPS

MIKE AND RODERICK SHARE THE SAME THREE KEY leadership principles: relationships, relationships, and relationships (and, as Mike jokingly says, "in that order"). Their view is that whether in business, a crisis, or just life in general, success and failure come down to relationships.

In practice, this means relationships—both internal and external—need to be seen as a business and leadership strategy. You have to think about creating, strengthening, and maintaining relationships for the long term rather than as just a transactional task. This is especially true in a crisis.

Mike was hand-selected by the US military to take up a key posting in Pakistan following the earthquake. His name carried weight with the government, and it was all due to the relationships he had built. After his exemplary leadership during the

earthquake, he was seen as a trustworthy partner and representative of the United States government. While the bilateral
relationship was at times rocky, the Pakistanis knew that Mike
understood Pakistan and would be honest in his assessment.

*Closing ceremony at Qasim Air Base in Islamabad, Pakistan
where the Pakistani Air Base hosted all Operation Lifeline's
response rotary wing aircraft.*

Most importantly, when Mike made a promise, he kept it.
During the earthquake recovery, Mike worked alongside a
number of high-ranking officials. They saw firsthand how he
managed the crisis and kept Pakistan's interests in the fore-
front of his decision-making. When Mike said something
would be done, it was done. When he gave a deadline, he hit it.
No matter where you are in the world, or what industry you're
in, that kind of reliability is universal.

After the disaster, Mike was flown back to Pakistan for a special ceremony, at the invitation of President Musharraf. He was awarded the highest honor given to a foreign military officer: the *Hilal-i-Quaid-i-Azam* (Order of Great Leader), and members of Mike's team who participated in the earthquake relief were awarded the *Sitara-i-Eisaar* (Star of Sacrifice). These were symbols of a mutual respect and trust that had been hard-earned over the past years. He knew many of his Pakistani counterparts by name. Because of his previous work, these leaders respected Mike and what he did for Pakistan.

Mike's relationship with Pakistan helped to build a foundation for US diplomacy, provide an inroad for NGOs and humanitarian organizations, and create a trusted network for coordinated operations with the International Security Assistance Forces (ISAF) and counterterrorism operations. All of it came down to Mike's commitment to building relationships.

IT'S ALL ABOUT TRUST

In the dead of night on May 2, 2011, two helicopters flew low over Abbottabad, Pakistan. Inside were highly trained SEALs, the US military's elite of the elite, and they had a singular mission: capture or kill Usama bin Laden.

When President Obama announced the news hours later, Pakistan was understandably upset, as the US had operated in complete secrecy. If Pakistan had wanted, it could have kicked out all US personnel, jeopardizing the mission in Afghanistan, regional counterterrorism operations, and the bilateral relationship. These were difficult times, and Mike was one of the few people who the Pakistanis would talk to during these very tense weeks based on the trust Mike built up over the years.

The relationship was strong enough to endure this great stress because of Mike's emphasis on the key elements of trust: following through on his promises, maintaining consistency in his relationship, focusing on the win-win, and checking his organizational ego at the door.

Building and maintaining relationships during a crisis is critical. Everyone has their own agendas and stressors, and you have to bring them into alignment. At Concentric, we often created relationship maps that helped us visualize the connections between our clients, employers, and stakeholders.

Similar to an Org Chart, a Relationship Map demonstrates with lines and color-coding the various ways that people within your sphere are connected. Do these two vendors often work together? Is there bad blood between this client and that one? By having this mapped out and updated at all times, you'll have a potent tool in your belt to navigate your relationships and position yourself closer to your end game.

Once you recognize that a situation has developed into a crisis, it's important to visualize all the lifelines you'll need and start looking for ones you don't have yet. If you haven't started building up those relationships, now is the time.

CHECKING YOUR EGO

When Mike landed in Pakistan, he brought with him the might of the US military. There is literally no other entity capable of bringing to bear the manpower, resources, and heavy lift. He could have bulldozed every organization and acted like the big kid on the block, but that wouldn't have served any real purpose other than an ego boost. In fact, it would have put off other organizations, stressed an already anxious host nation, and hurt relations globally.

It's important to remember that ego, in the context of leading an organization, is in no way a bad thing. One of your responsibilities is to champion, and defend, your team. If you *don't* have an ego, you can be drowned out by louder voices. Yet you need to keep the mission in mind. Your end game is a goal for your entire organization, not just you as an individual. To reach that goal, you need to set aside your own ambitions and check your personal and professional ego at the door.

This also means watching out for the egos of others. Mike met with a General in Pakistan who had requested a CH-47 for a trip to visit his forces. This wasn't a bad person, and they weren't wasting resources intentionally. They just saw themselves and the importance of the trip through a different lens. It was a mindset that required a simple course correction in that the needs and the capability of the Chinook was needed more to deliver the 10,000 pounds of supplies to other locations.

It is a challenge at times to manage personalities, but it's a part of building a coalition during a crisis. This may be one of the hardest hurdles to overcome when working on relationships.

BUILDING AUTHENTIC RELATIONSHIPS

As with mental wellness and resiliency, building a relationship requires authenticity. There are hundreds of books written about forging new relationships, but we believe it all boils down to one thing: curiosity. If you want to connect to someone in an authentic way, you need to bring, and seek, the gift of information.

Admiral LeFever, in his role as Commander, Office of Defense Representative Pakistan (ODRP) reuniting with General Ashfaq Kayani, then Chief of Army Staff, in 2008.

No matter where you travel, you will discover nuances of different cultures. Mike had spent time in the Middle East, but he hadn't studied up on the history or peoples of Pakistan. As he sat with local leaders, he discovered wonderful facts and insight on the culture. They were curious about the rest of the world and had the same desires we all want for our families. Mike learned about the Pakistani commitment to family and tribe, to region and religion. Now separated from the chaos of the earthquake, communities opened their doors and arms to welcome the helping hands from across the world.

Authentic connection is about **shared goals, clear communication, and feedback**. For communication, you need to ensure that you are understood, and that you understand what is being presented to you. Feedback is equally important, whether positive or negative. It's unlikely that someone on your team will have a perfect run and never need any kind of criticism, but you as a leader need to be tactful with how you share feedback. Praise can be delivered at any time and is best when done in public. Let others see what happens when they perform admirably. Constructive feedback should be delivered in private, and we do emphasize the "constructive" part.

Mike returned to Washington, DC at various times to debrief with key leaders in the government and military. After an important meeting with the National Security Council there was a moment that Mike will always remember. The President, on a busy schedule, was ushered out of this meeting and

onto his next one. A few moments later the President came
back into the room and approached Mike and said: "Hey,
I always see you on the other end of the screen [the virtual
conference], and it's great to see you in person. I can't thank
you enough for what you're doing in Pakistan," and then he
went on to his schedule.

*Admiral LeFever meeting with 46th Vice President Dick Cheney
on December 20, 2005 during his visit to MASH 212 in Muzaffarabad, Pakistan.*

When you've been in the military as long as Mike had, you
receive more than your share of "attaboys." Still, few things
compare to the Commander in Chief personally compliment-
ing your work and effort. Never underestimate the power of
praise.

RELATIONSHIPS, RELATIONSHIPS, RELATIONSHIPS

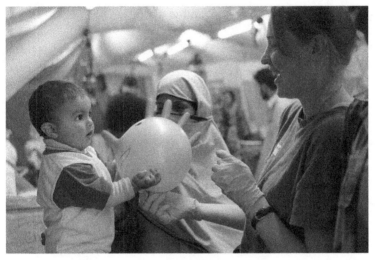

Sailors and Marines distracting and playing with the Pakistani children while they were being triaged for care at the MASH.

A crisis is going to test your relationships more than anything else. It is a chance to show your friends, your team, and competition just what you're made of. Don't be afraid of the changes that come, just know where you are going and who you want to take with you.

- Make sure you are building trust on both sides of any relationship, and don't give yours away without confidence it is returned

- Check your ego and remember that your end game is the main goal

- Be authentic and curious as you build new relationships

- Give as much as you gain in a relationship

KEEP THE DOOR OPEN

It is important to decide how vital relationships are to you, your business, and your management of a crisis. If people know you, it's less likely they'll just say "no" flat out. A relationship is a powerful tool that will keep you moving forward in the most dire of times.

Start building relationships from a place of authenticity and trust. Don't overpromise, and make sure you're ready to take on responsibilities so you can make a proper impression. Keep in mind the little things, and go the extra mile to show that you care and respect the person on the other side.

Relationships have been key in every critical decision that we had to make in our careers. Both in and out of a crisis, we have opted to secure the long-term advantage of a relationship over the short-term gains of another choice. Make sure you understand the macro effects of any relationship on your personal and professional life. Of all the factors we've discussed in this book, relationships might be the most important in the long term.

CHAPTER 9

THE CRISIS
BALANCE SHEET

EVERY END GAME INCLUDES AN EXIT STRATEGY. AFTER
working hard to manage the crisis and position yourself for
the future, it's time to leave the chaos behind and return
to a normal operating tempo. Your team will resume their
intended functions, relationships will evolve, and you can
finally begin the work that you set out to do in the first place.
Of course, there is one final step that cannot be avoided: you
have to pay the bills.

As Mike prepared to leave Pakistan, he found himself star-
ing at pages and pages of equipment and resource manifests.
Over the course of the crisis, his team had built hospitals,
schools, supply caches, shelters, tents, and support for the

countless refugees. There were construction and heavy-lift vehicles, excess equipment, and a laundry list of miscellaneous items. Attached to every line was a price tag.

Vice Admiral LeFever signing over equipment to Pakistani Air Base during the 2010 flood response effort.

Any job, even one associated with a worldwide humanitarian effort, comes at a cost. Resources, labor, and material aren't free. The end game for Pakistan was, of course, to provide humanitarian assistance and improve US–Pakistan relations. Any decision Mike made with regards to the mission had to bring him closer to that end game. So when it came time to decide what to do with the resources—to either retrograde the equipment back to the US military or give it to Pakistan to support continuing efforts—the answer was simple: Mike worked with the DoD and obtained Congressional approval to allow the heavy construction equipment, the

MASH hospital, and forward refueling stations and equipment to remain with the host country.

By framing the exchange of resources as a part of the mission, it had more structure and symbolism with the Pakistani government as the United States' continued support for a friend in need. Islamabad was able to show its citizens that the government would spare no expense in procuring the finest material and equipment for the rebuilding effort. The US was able to demonstrate altruism on an international scale. It was a win-win for the mission. However, not all debts are paid right away.

Years later, as helicopters flew over Pakistan carrying Navy SEALs and the body of Usama bin Laden, a new cost applied to the international debt. While not a fiscal matter, the goodwill cost of a covert operation was substantial. No country wants to learn about an incursion after the fact, especially considering the circumstances. Pakistan, whether knowingly or unknowingly, had been a harbor for the most wanted man in the world. In the cold light of day, an extensive bill appeared that required immediate action.

Mike's efforts in both the earthquake and the flood had bought America a significant amount of goodwill with Pakistan, and much of that was spent following the bin Laden raid. It would take months of careful diplomatic action to resume ties, but that bridge could have been impossible to rebuild without an initial relationship forged through both the flood, earthquake responses, and a host of other significant engagements and cooperation.

Debt is a literal and hypothetical bill that covers a huge number of factors, and you need to understand how it affects you before, during, and after a crisis.

THE STARTUP MINDSET

When you start a business, you understand that you likely won't see a profit for eighteen months or more. This launch period is very similar to a crisis, which is why a crisis mindset can be compared to a startup mindset. You have to make quick, difficult decisions in order to keep yourself moving. You accrue debt with only the plan of recovery in the future.

When a crisis hits a startup, it doesn't have the luxury of weathering the storm. Drastic measures are often taken to keep the business afloat. This could mean selling off ownership of the company in the form of shares in order to raise money. Losing 10 percent of your company is a calculated risk so long as you still have a company at the end of the crisis.

You might find yourself in a financial pit with no clear means of climbing out. This is a difficult situation, and it requires some painful triage of your company. You'll need to take a brutal look at which assets you can stand to lose. Selling off equipment and cutting overhead is never an enviable position. It can feel like a step backward. But you have to keep in mind that your responsibility as the owner is to the company and your team. If you don't make a decision and the business fails, you lose more than just bits and pieces. Bringing in an outside investor might not have been in your initial plan, but if it keeps you in the orange (operating in debt), it still brings you closer to your end game.

When you use debt as a tool for crisis management, you need to look at all of your funding options. While each brings its own pros and cons, you have to consider how they will affect your goals. Remember that surviving a crisis is about more than just financial success.

Even major businesses have to consider outside support from time to time. Billion-dollar companies took government support during the pandemic. This way, they were able to continue paying their staff despite a major loss in customers and revenue. It's a debt that will take time to repay, but it's far better than losing the business altogether.

Debt, in the simplest terms, is a promise of future repayment. If you take out a loan at a bank, you incur a debt that often comes with interest. That's why a bank is willing to lend you money. When you understand that debt encompasses the future of your business, you can see how that future repayment can be a part of your end game.

Taking on debt allows you to maintain control over your situation in the short term. With interest rates low, this is a useful vehicle to manage a crisis. Anything that lessens your monthly stressor is a good tool to keep in your belt. However, debt is a double-edged sword. Just as it can be a path out of a crisis, it can exacerbate an already difficult situation. When used wisely, this is a tool that you can use to navigate your situation, and it can help you position yourself and your company for growth. Understanding how to use debt takes time and practice, which is why you shouldn't wait for a crisis to plan on your future.

ACCRUING DEBT

As soon as a crisis begins, the debt begins to accrue. In order for you to successfully navigate the uncertainty and urgency, you need to have a firm understanding of your budget. This is one reason we commonly compare crisis management to a startup mindset. In both instances, you need to be granular about monitoring your finances.

Of course, debt in this regard isn't solely about finances. Mike's efforts during the flood and earthquake had left the US with nearly 70 percent approval in the region; however, that increase was short-lived. If they fell too far, that could lead to a geopolitical crisis in an already contested region. We've spoken about the importance of relationships before, but you have to understand that debt applies to connections on a personal and professional level as well.

If you own a business, you have a baseline of operating costs. There's overhead, salaries, and benefits that have to be paid whether you make any money or not. In a crisis, those bills don't just stop. In fact, they may increase due to any number of factors. If you're unprepared to manage your budget and make difficult choices, you'll quickly run out of capital.

At the same time, you are not experiencing a crisis in a vacuum. All around you, other people and other businesses have to weather the same storm. By understanding how debt can actually serve your needs, and act as collateral in a business environment, you'll open up new avenues to creatively solve your follow-on problems. At the onset of a crisis, despite what your instincts may say, be ready to *spend* resources. Making swift purchases early on can forestall a greater crisis down the road and position you to exit the disaster even better than before.

Finally, understand that a crisis will balloon debt faster than you've seen under normal circumstances. You have to prepare yourself for the reality of that growth, otherwise you risk being completely overwhelmed at the end game. This includes personal costs, relationships, and professional reputations.

Debt is all-encompassing, but it isn't something to fear. Rather, you need to work on comprehension so that you can use debt to your advantage. And, as always, keep your end game in mind. If the debt you're taking on doesn't support your goals, it might just be wasteful spending.

FUNDING METHOD

Regardless of the crisis you face, you will need resources in order to survive. This means understanding your funding method—how are you going to acquire the funds necessary to operate until the end of the crisis? Remember that not all methods are created equal, and some might go in the complete opposite direction from your end game.

While there are variations, it boils down to two options: Take on Investors, or Take on Debt.

When you're starting up a business, you may choose to reach out to investors to raise capital. In return, you offer ownership of your company with the aim to return that investment through profits down the road. Investors generally understand that they are assuming some risk in order to potentially see a windfall. However, investors may not always agree with your intentions for the business. Their end game might not be aligned with yours. Consider Mike and the coalition. There were many countries and organizations working in tandem on the recovery, but that also meant a lot of personalities to manage in order to keep the group focused on the task at hand.

In a serious crisis, you will often find offers that pull at ownership of your company piecemeal. You'll sell off one percent here, two percent there, and suddenly you're working a sixteen-hour day for a company that you don't even own. If you do manage to weather the crisis and emerge at your end game, you hardly get to reap any of the profits.

Taking on debt allows you to operate alone, as the bank loaning you capital isn't likely to start offering unsolicited business advice. This allows you autonomy and the potential for a larger financial win once your company becomes profitable.

The risk is much higher on a default, as there is no backup to help you out of a financial crisis.

Funding is situationally dependent. You can't just plug in a formula and expect to come out on top. Just as your business is unique, the funding method you choose should be as well.

THE SECONDARY EFFECTS OF DEBT

There are no guarantees in a crisis, and you can do everything right and still end up deeper in debt. At that point, you might consider more drastic options. You could raise money by selling off assets or reducing staff. We would highly suggest that this be considered a method of last resort. Aside from the severe morale cost, there are second and third order effects that you'll suffer by sacrificing resources and personnel.

Reducing staff is a stopgap, and it comes at a cost. You lower your overhead but also reduce your capacity. If you lose an employee with a unique skill, you've either lost a capability or just added a new debt to hire someone else. Staff cuts also bring a heavy loss to morale, and a crisis is already a test of your team's mental fortitude.

Your responsibility as a business owner is to your people. They accepted the risk when they came to work with you, and you owe them the trust they have placed in you. We found ourselves in a similar situation with Concentric, but we knew our business couldn't survive without the hardworking team we had built.

Selling off assets, such as equipment or remote office spaces, can be a quick source of income. However, this won't be a recurring revenue stream, and it still lowers your capacity. If your end game is about expansion for your company, then this step is directly in opposition to your goals.

Losing ground to investors comes with its own cost. Remember, relationship debt (or reputation debt) is a very real expense. Roderick often realized that he'd lost leverage with investors because of previous transactions and conversations. The decisions made under a previous crisis had a direct impact on the current one.

Whichever method you choose, research the explicit and hidden costs associated with the funding. What are you gaining by moving down this path, and what is at risk? How much do you stand to lose if you default? And before you make any decision, you need to identify the resources you have and endure the crisis.

IDENTIFYING YOUR RESOURCES

The first question you need to ask yourself is how much it costs to run your business. We're not just talking about finances either. This is a crucial part of budgeting both before and during a crisis. What resources do you need in order to be successful day to day, week to week, and so on toward your end game? We encountered this when facing our crisis at Concentric. We faced a potential loss of 40 percent of our business, which meant we wouldn't be able to afford our daily operating costs as they were. It required a rapid evolution of our business in order to overcome this sudden challenge.

First, we start with the baseline: what are the unchanging costs of day-to-day operation? This includes renting a space, utilities, and any equipment that is either leased or purchased. If we cannot afford these costs, then we need to immediately examine our funding method. We can't exactly sell the building in order to recoup a few dollars.

Next, we need to look at our operating costs. When the business is open, what expenses are accrued? This is an area where we can make small and large adjustments to create resources. In any case, this number is more flexible, but still necessary in order to run our business.

Finally, we need a staff to help serve our customers. We need to identify our minimum staff required in order to fulfill our maximum potential. Once you've identified your operating costs, now look at your worst-case scenarios. What is the minimum daily goal for customer sales needed in order to keep running?

Knowing your resources is also about your staff. They are far more precious resources than simple capital, and they offer advantages in the midst of a crisis. Mike often found that his team was invaluable in finding creative solutions to complex problems during the rescue effort. As he worked alongside these professionals, Mike began to find hidden talents that could be put to work toward the end game. Similarly, Mike and Roderick worked with their team of talent to evolve their services in response to the COVID-19 international travel shutdown.

Once you understand your resources, you'll be able to see the bigger picture. A crisis is a challenge but also an opportunity. It all depends on how you approach the problem.

MACRO CONTEXT, MICRO ISSUES

As a leader, you have to learn how to view your situation from both a micro and macro perspective. You will face problems that affect only the small scale: the sudden loss of a key employee, a vendor going out of business that makes a critical component. These instances create small crises, but they won't affect the larger picture. A macro incident could be an earthquake, a pandemic, or a stock market crash. Everyone, including your competition, is in the same boat.

Navigating a crisis means recognizing the connections between micro and macro. Your small business might not affect the larger effort during a natural disaster, but the disaster certainly has an impact on you. At the same time, while you're focused on managing the crisis for your business, your employees have micro issues of their own. Their personal financial situation connects to your business as well.

When you prepare a plan to manage the debt during a crisis, you need to consider how this will affect the world above and below your perspective. At Concentric, we took a risk pivoting into a domestic market. We had to consider how this would affect our staff, as well as the impact it could have on customers and competition. It was important to focus on our end game, but we couldn't ignore the cascading effects of our decisions.

Situational awareness will only aid you in managing the crisis. If you know what is happening around you, then the path toward your end game becomes clearer.

THE DEBT OF THE END GAME

Ambassador Crocker and Mike sat down to look over the situation in Pakistan. Even before the earthquake, resources were often restricted in distant areas, requiring complex—and expensive—logistical solutions. They saw an opportunity to not only rebuild the nation, but to bring it to a place better than it had been before. With the resources available for a global humanitarian effort, Mike and Ambassador Crocker saw a path toward larger, loftier goals than they could have achieved without the crisis.

As Mike left Pakistan for the last time, he saw a country transformed by a global effort. Twice over, the world had pooled its resources to help out a neighbor and friend during a disaster, leaving Pakistan stronger in areas than before the crisis began. The US achieved its end game of a closer relationship, and Pakistan achieved its end game of a more prosperous nation.

In a crisis, you have to keep your eye on the bigger picture and your larger goals. You *will* be coming out of this, so how are you preparing to come out successfully? Taking on new debts is an inevitability; the bill starts the moment the calamity begins. Are you spending so much now that you've created the conditions for failure after the crisis?

You need to understand the debt instruments you are using; they have terms, and they will come due before long. While a loan is a viable vehicle so long as interest rates are low, defaulting can have drastic consequences. Understand your limitations, so you don't snatch defeat from the jaws of victory.

A crisis doesn't happen in isolation. The debts earned in the earthquake paid off in international relationships during the bin Laden raid, and Mike's service is still a boon used to keep channels open with Pakistan. The good you do during your own crisis will build on relationships and pathways that can lead you toward your end game.

Make sure you understand your resources before a crisis begins, and that members of your team know the roles that they play in the bigger picture. When you have confidence in your ability to weather a crisis, you are more likely to emerge successful.

Now that you've made it this far in the book, look back on everything you've learned. How much did you know, or *think* you knew, before you began? What lessons have you learned that you need to keep moving forward? It's time to consider how you continue your education when the crisis is finally over.

CHAPTER 10

THE FEEDBACK LOOP

IN THE MILITARY, EVERY EXERCISE AND MISSION—NO matter how small—is followed by an After Action Review, or AAR. This is a chance for every member of the unit to discuss the event, breaking down actions they want to improve and others they want to sustain. Then, the next time they are planning a similar mission, the unit can sit down with their notes and practice how to perform better the next time.

As flood waters overran bridges in 2008, the Pakistani Chief of Army Staff Ashfaq Parvez Kayani contacted Mike and Ambassador Patterson. "Remember those halal MREs you brought out here last time? It would be a good idea to start packing because this flood is more severe than we thought."

In the aftermath of the earthquake and Operation Lifeline, Mike brought a battle staff that had just completed the Brightstar training exercise. Now, years later, Mike had a different group of officers and NCOs to bring along for a rescue operation.

They spent their short build-up time going over the notes from the last disaster. Mike's team had each conducted an AAR of their own units, providing detailed instructions for logistics, heavy lift, medical, and infrastructure repair in the region. Mike had the knowledge from the last disaster for the types of supplies and resources that would be needed to support the country. They were as prepared as they could be, but they also knew that their plans might not fit the reality on the ground.

Most of the plans from the earthquake were still viable, setting Mike and his team well ahead of where he'd been only a few years before. With prior knowledge at their fingertips, they were able to scale their disaster relief operations as needed. Yet even with all this experience, a monumental challenge loomed. In the earthquake, there were roughly 3.5 million Pakistanis left homeless. After the floods, it was closer to 60 million.

AFTER THE ACTION, WHAT'S NEXT?

A crisis will eventually run its course. No matter the outcome, it is important to sit down with your team and conduct an AAR as soon as possible while the actions and details are fresh in your mind. The US military conducts an AAR after every significant action—whether it is in response to an event, a planned mission, or a training exercise—to document the learning from everyone involved to inform future planning, training, decision-making, and even organizational change.

The most important part of being a learning organization is a continuous focus on a commitment to improvement. The AAR enables that by examining these aspects: what went well and why it went well, regardless of success or failure; and what is needed to improve in the future, especially in responding to the unexpected. An AAR is not a blame game; it is focused on reflection, how we could do better, and how to capitalize on opportunities we only realized in hindsight.

The bottom line: a crisis is the ultimate teacher, and if we aren't learning from it, we risk repeating the same mistakes. We can learn as much in a few months of a crisis as entire years in normal circumstances.

An After Action Review is a formal, specific, and documented process. If you don't **write it down**, it's far too easy to forget. Once you have these notes, you can **devise a plan** for the next crisis, so you won't make the same mistakes. Then you need to assign someone to actually **develop these new ideas**, and you should incorporate them into your ongoing training. Before the next crisis, you'll drill this new behavior so that it is tested and ready for the next time you need it.

This is a group activity, something that involves every level of your organization. If you assign this as a task to just one or two people, you risk losing all of that gained knowledge from everyone just when you need it most. By limiting the people involved, you also risk missing out on key events that weren't witnessed by those in leadership positions. Also, by involving everyone and focusing on transparency and sharing, it builds greater team awareness and is a great trust—and team—building activity.

This is one of the things we did with Concentric that was incredibly impactful. You have to be relentlessly focused on getting feedback. It's not just you as a leader; it is creating a culture of learning and anticipating the future. There's a tendency in a crisis to become reactive, and so often we forget to take stock of what we're doing and why we're doing it.

When you've created this feedback loop, partially from formal AARs, you will grow as an institution. The knowledge of past successes and mistakes develops into confidence, enabling even bolder decisions in the future.

BREAKING DOWN AN AFTER ACTION REVIEW

In simple terms, an AAR is a discussion of the entirety of the event. You want to start from the very beginning, looking at the lead-up to the crisis, the actions taken during, the resources utilized, the personnel and positions required, and the way you transitioned to a more normal operating cadence.

Gather everyone who was involved to get their honest feedback. As we said, you want views from the top of your organization all the way to the most junior employee. In fact, a lot of the best insight comes from the people closest to the problem sets or the impact of the crisis.

An AAR is an honest, critical assessment focused on improvement for the future. It isn't an excuse to point fingers or undercut colleagues or the boss. As a leader, it is all about creating the environment for candid and constructive feedback and the ability to speak up without fear of negative judgment or reaction. To keep the discussion flowing, it should be led and moderated. Assign someone to take notes—although everyone present should anyways—and someone else to keep track of time. Then follow a simple format: what happened, what should we improve, what should we sustain, and what happened that we did not anticipate?

What Happened?

The leader of the review leads the discussion to capture the actual timeline and detail of events as they unfolded. This is meant to be a straightforward discussion, so reserve any judgment as everyone weighs in with their perspectives. It can help to write down your thoughts ahead of time so you can stay focused and detailed.

Find a natural flow for describing how one event led to another. Often you'll be able to highlight key decision points that altered the course for the organization. It also may be helpful to break up the conversation into sections so you can cover each topic in detail. This will also prevent you from missing out on key feedback areas by rushing through the story.

What Should We Improve?

No matter how well-trained your organization might be, mistakes will be made. You'll likely find key decisions that caused undesirable consequences, processes that lagged or collapsed under pressure, roles and responsibilities that did not fit the new circumstances or were missing. Mark those down as important discussion topics and allow the group to pick apart what could have been done differently and to identify what needs to be revised, tightened up, discarded, created, or better planned for.

Improvements should focus on building a process and more agile frameworks for the future rather than an action. When you build a system with a single point of failure, it only takes one bad decision to undo all of your hard work. Instead, look at how you can place safeties into your procedures to prevent those same consequences from happening again. If discussion bogs down on individual actions (or inactions) or focuses only on mistakes, redirect the focus to the results of the mistake and turn the discussion toward the process.

Most important of all, ensure that any solutions discussed during the AAR are written down. A million-dollar idea doesn't net you anything if you forget it the next day.

What Should We Sustain?

The question of what to sustain also focuses on the process and desired outcomes, not the person. It is not who did what, but what actions were taken that contributed to the desired outcomes—and how to ensure they are repeatable or amplified for future success. Even in failure, there are always things that went well, processes that worked, and roles and responsibilities that evolved as needed. The discussion on sustainability also helps to capture the key inflection points or signals for decision, action, or pivot to recognize in the next crisis.

We found that it helps to end the discussion on sustainability. Your team has just endured a crisis, and these talks can be difficult. There is a lot of honest feedback that emerges from an AAR, and it is never desirable to head back to work after a gut punch. Instead, end the day with a major victory and congratulate everyone on a job well done.

INCORPORATING LESSONS LEARNED

When Mike was the Captain of a Destroyer, he held his AARs with everyone on the bridge of the ship. On a ten thousand-ton vessel, there were hundreds of people running around and performing intricate tasks, sailing in restricted waters to pull into port. It was a complex evolution involving every aspect of the ship and its crew. During the first few AAR discussions, the officers and NCOs were hesitant to call out any mistakes. Mike would often joke, "Oh, everything went that well?"

In his AARs, Mike would go around the room to ensure everyone contributed to the discussion, often giving his junior members the most space to talk. He created an environment for all members of his team—to include the most junior personnel—to share on processes that could be improved. In fact, the closer to the action the person was, the more focused their criticism and input.

We made AARs as a matter of routine at Concentric. It became part of our operational cadence, especially after the pandemic hit. We also ensured that AAR outcomes were used to inform future planning and execution. This included everything from a supported trip, to a big proposal, to routine processes. The more we worked this process into our tempo, the more its value was realized. We took our lessons learned, our solutions for future improvement, and actually put them into practice.

The work doesn't stop with an AAR; if anything, that's when the work begins. This means coming up with an actual plan to build these lessons into your processes. It means assigning responsibility within your team. Most of all, it means follow-up on your part.

We found it helps to break down the AAR results into two fields: Tactical and Procedural. A tactical fix is simple. Someone pressed a button when they weren't supposed to, which caused a problem. We make it so you can't press that button, or we implement safeties so the button can only be pressed once the right conditions are met. It is a single fix for a critical component.

A procedural fix requires a bit more care. Frequently it means interrupting a normal process to insert new steps, add in details, and build safeties that prevent an undesirable outcome. Procedural fixes often need to be tested. If you want to change your sales process in order to remove points of failure and ensure quality control at each step, you can't test that in a vacuum. It requires a second evaluation.

A PHD IN FAILURE

Roderick's cybersecurity startup failed in October 2020 after about five years of work. It was a difficult and humbling experience, but a necessary one. He always wondered, *If we had done X, would it have led to Y?* He explored those results again and again, and concluded that the point of failure had been limited resources. As a leader, Roderick couldn't help but see the opportunity from this review. He spent six months alone, hunched over his notes and a computer, essentially earning a PhD in how he'd failed. It helped him prepare for the future but also demonstrated the value of self-critique.

An AAR is almost like getting your PhD in resiliency. You're going to have the insight and the emotional distance from it to accept objective truths. Our AAR wasn't a pity party, although we certainly could have let it become one. Instead, we started experimenting with how we could have done things better and identifying what steps were missing and/or needed to be improved for future success.

We came up with a new plan, an evolution of the business model that informed Concentric's strategic thinking. At the end of that AAR, we had pages of notes detailing each area where we had some success, and others where things did not go well or failed. It felt like we had figured out the formula, but now we needed to evaluate once again, to try things out, make sure things held together, whether our decided innovation and improvement appreciably made things better.

The second evaluation comes after a few weeks or months have passed. This is when you take out your notes and run a drill on the new process. Test your theories to see if they hold water. If you came up with a new sales technique, run it past a client. If you have a production pipeline, walk through one time with your key leaders. Work with your employees to help ensure they are actually able to accomplish what was decided and, if the "new" and "better" isn't working, to provide the resources and opportunity to iterate some more. It is always beneficial to follow through and track the outcomes of decisions and improvements made to ensure they are value-added and—if not—to trust the input of those who are closest to the work to help course correct.

When you look at your ideas in the cold light of day, do they work? Be honest. If not, there's no shame. But better to find out now, on your terms and your timeline, than during the next crisis. Remember that an AAR is about data collection, and you can incorporate this new bit of information into your next planning session. You'll be able to come up with even better ideas, and you will find the path forward that works.

AFTER THE DISASTER

Setting up a formal review process takes little time and effort, but it pays dividends for your organization. Make this a positive change in your company, and remember:

- Conduct reviews immediately after the crisis ends, so the event is fresh

- Assign roles during the AAR and lead the discussion yourself

- Describe what happened, what went right, and what can be improved

- Put these lessons into practice, and learn from your mistakes

Mike had the knowledge from the earthquake to help his team respond to a flooded Pakistan. This enabled them to use tested procedures when planning out the recovery effort. They didn't need to reinvent the wheel, and that saved time, resources, and lives.

Once the initial chaos passed, Mike was able to bring leaders from each group together to share their insights and review lessons learned. They discussed their successes and failures in an open and honest way, looking for the right path toward the end game rather than a chance to earn credit and clout.

As the weeks passed, they tested their theories and learned even better ways of performing their tasks, which they documented for future teams. They created systems that would save lives in crises around the world. Indeed, the Pakistan humanitarian disaster relief experiences are now the teaching standard for US training for both military and civilians.

Reflection is a key part of growth. It helps teams and organizations not only learn from success, mistake, and failure, but also, critically, to recognize what is working and capitalize on that success. It promotes understanding of—and confidence in—how to navigate through and adapt to new circumstances.

CHAPTER 11

UNDERCURRENTS

THE CHANGES DIDN'T HAPPEN OVERNIGHT, BUT THEY arrived with force nonetheless. When the earthquake hit, remote areas were suddenly exposed to medical care, nutrition and other services, and international support for education and training that they had not previously experienced at such scale. It was a rapid development, and not without consequences.

International organizations assisted in helping residents build back better: constructing houses rated for future earthquakes, introducing farming equipment and techniques for increased overall crop yields, and teaching women and children new skills for improved lifestyle. Proper medical care, nutrition, and shelters had a profound impact on the devastated area, with the region experiencing its lowest mortality rate on record.

Pakistan and US logo items were very effective in promoting the partnership of the two nations.

None of this was offered with any sort of mal-intent; Mike wasn't out to change a culture. But, as he discovered, the actions taken throughout the crisis created changes to the area that would impact it for some time.

As the Pakistani government took over, many of the talks centered on how life could return to "normal." How had the US and international relief organizations' presence in the region left a lasting impact on the people? And how much was sustainable by the host government?

What happens when the crisis is over and the "angels of mercy" leave?

THE FUTURE ISN'T EVENLY DISTRIBUTED

Have you ever been to a beach and been pulled along by the undertow? When it's strong, you'll feel the water tugging you away from the shore. It's easy to know when you should turn back, or at least close distance. However, if the undertow is subtle, you might suddenly find yourself hundreds of feet away from where you started.

When a crisis arrives, the status quo is permanently altered. No matter the scale, a crisis creates and accelerates socio-economic change throughout the affected area. Sometimes currents are obvious, and you can spot them coming from miles away. Other times, you won't notice the undercurrents until they've changed your world forever. As author William Gibson said, "The future is already here—it's just not very evenly distributed."

Undercurrents are potential energy. They already exist, and in many cases are already moving in a direction. The crisis simply adds more momentum to the situation. If a market was heading for a crash, it would topple over the edge. If a society is trending toward a new form of government, a crisis opens the door for a revolution. You can't stop the undercurrent; you just have to learn to swim with, through, or across it.

Even better is learning to recognize the signs of the under-current. Remember, the purpose of crisis management is understanding your end game. You have a goal to work toward, and the world may or may not support your decisions. If you can sense how the landscape is shifting, you can use that knowledge to your advantage as you plot a path forward.

If you're paying attention, you'll notice at least some signs early on. During the height of the COVID-19 lockdowns, for example, we suddenly realized that we weren't using paper money all that often. The more people we asked, the more they agreed that they preferred using a credit card or simply tapping their phone against a tablet. Knowing this, it wasn't all that surprising to see cryptocurrency take advantage of the shifting perception of how finances could be spent.

Think back twenty or thirty years. How comfortable were people with making large purchases over the phone? More often than not, customers needed to see a product in their hands before shelling out the big bucks. Now, after years of digitization, people can buy cars using an app on their phone. With COVID-19 forcing many people to rethink trips out, almost every good you can imagine is now available at the push of a button. The undercurrent was always there, with more and more people willing to buy something sight unseen. The crisis simply made it a necessity and accelerated the change.

How can you recognize the changes that exist in your industry? Which ones will be affected by the current crisis? And most importantly, how do you position yourself to take advantage of a changing market?

THE SUBTLE SHIFTS

Take a look at your business, at your industry. Where is it headed in the next five years? How about the next ten? Are you actively preparing for that evolution, or is it something that you've put off for another day? Remember that, in a crisis, those changes have a tendency to accelerate.

In a crisis, that five-year plan might come due in less than a year. Those subtle changes that you've been tracking will evolve into a landslide. Blockbuster didn't consider Netflix a threat because the internet was still in its infancy. Arcades didn't consider home computers and consoles a threat because the systems couldn't compete for power. Then, when the tides turned with technology, these older companies couldn't keep up. Since they hadn't prepared for the evolution to begin with, they were left behind as others took their place.

Think about how Netflix rode the undercurrents to assume its place at the top. The current model when they first arrived was a physical retail location with a limited selection of movies to rent. Netflix provided a disruptive plan to mail you movies directly—even including a return envelope to keep the process seamless. In response to continual shifts, they adopted a subscription model to keep customers coming back and then evolved to a digital-only subscription, correctly anticipating advances in internet speeds and streaming content. Now, the company is once again threatened by undercurrents: pressure to give creators more control and the looming streaming wars.

Understanding the shifting currents underneath your business is crucial for survival. At Concentric, for example, we constantly consider all kinds of scenarios relating to security and drones— from household alarm systems to new ways of delivering toxic bombs and a market fueled by consumers enjoying the novelty of a flying camera. However, after ten years of adoption and experimentation, drone technology is beginning to have some of those serious uses for security. The near-disposable cost of the hardware—combined with the arrival of more sophisticated software, which includes an element of AI—is creating the market for security-threatening drones much like we had foreseen. As we think about the pandemic crisis and the rise in domestic crime, it seems likely drones will play an ever-increasing role in policing and security. Only by keeping our radar sharp were we able to stay ahead of this undercurrent.

How can you identify the trends moving underneath your industry? What should you look for? As we found in our research, it's all about tuning your radar.

TUNING YOUR RADAR

In order to understand the undercurrents in your market, you need to be informed. This means developing a proper "thinking network" to help you figure out what's going on in your industry and where things might head in the future.

Tuning your radar in this instance means finding the key milestones that demonstrate change occurring around you. It is stepping outside your normal operating space and keeping abreast of events that could have second and third order effects on your networks. It's hard to know when you've become too comfortable with your current situation to objectively step outside of it. That's why you need more eyes and ears seeking out undercurrents. If you miss it, someone else has a chance to catch it.

Being an informed leader, as with gathering intelligence, is all about finding trustworthy sources of information and networks of people. One of the best ways to stay informed is to talk to people on the ground. In this regard, your employees are an excellent resource for identifying undercurrents. Your frontline salesperson will know faster than anyone how a product is moving or what clients are asking for. Your warehouse manager can tell you which vendors are struggling to fill orders, which could demonstrate a supply blockage that will affect the whole industry.

It can be invaluable to have your team share the mindset that the industry is always in flux. If everyone is watching for undercurrents, there is a smaller chance that you'll miss the change before it is too late to act.

Stepping out of your comfort zone can show you new paths forward that you might not have noticed otherwise.

IS YOUR BUSINESS PREPARED TO ADAPT?

In the first two months of COVID-19, we sat down to evaluate our company's viability. Security as an industry is fairly customer-centric in order to attain that trust dynamic. If you can't be with the customer to develop that rapport, how can you provide the same level of service? We had to address which aspects of our business could adapt to a virtual environment and which required new safety measures to adapt to COVID-19 restrictions.

We sat down with a client in December of 2019 to discuss our services. Over the course of the conversation, we inevitably landed on the "what ifs." How would we handle this type of attack, or a cyber strike, or DDoS. Then, somewhat prophetically, we talked about a potential pandemic. Granted, the circumstances were different (we looked at it from a bioterror perspective), but it gave us a moment to consider our own flexibility. How would we adapt to such a situation?

When we returned to the home office, we brought up these contingencies with the team. It became a standard brainstorming session. We would go around and try out various scenarios to see where our blind spots might be. It was a stress test for our viability to adapt, and it's one of the reasons we were able to quickly act at the beginning of 2020.

We have always found success in—and sometimes been criticized for—engaging our teams in these hypothetical "what if" sessions. Building critical thinking skills into your company culture is a solid start. Think in terms of the Most Likely changes and the Most Dangerous or Disruptive changes. These exercises help you prepare options well in advance of a crisis, and ensure you can stay ahead of trends.

Checking your company's flexibility relies on understanding your goals. If the undercurrent moves customers away from your primary service, does it make sense to chase after them if it's completely outside of your strategy and end game? Would it be better to restructure entirely? In our case, the undercurrents from COVID-19 prompted us to restructure to be able to be more aggressive in taking advantage of new avenues of revenue in this market.

Your viability depends on a large number of factors, and there is no way to prepare for every contingency. However, your ability to anticipate is greatly enhanced by bringing the full force of your company to watch for signs of change, design plans for adaptation, and practice what you'll do when your company needs to refit under duress. It might be that you cannot plan for every contingency, but you create the environment to be able to adapt ably to the changes.

Learning about undercurrents is just the first step. If you are building a successful company, you need to be sure it can adapt to changes in the industry. The way you prepare for evolution is by planning for it ahead of time. At the end of a crisis, all that matters is whether or not you met your end game goals. But if you can survive and still make a profit, you demonstrate that you prepared properly.

THE TIDES EBB AND FLOW

Change occurs whether you're ready for it or not. A crisis accelerates the currents that are already underneath your feet. By preparing now, you will know which moves to make to position yourself closer to your end game.

- Look at the current trends and discuss where you want to be now, before a crisis shortens the timeline

- When a crisis strikes, watch for subtle shifts and determine how they affect your intended end game

- Look at your business with a critical eye, and determine your viability for the changes that could come at any moment

Mike saw the undercurrents in Pakistan. The earthquake shook the very foundations of Pakistani society, leaving areas noticeably changed when the coalition left. The most significant foundational aspect was the sense that things could be better for those who had different perspectives on community essentials and collaboration. While a few things reverted back after the UN departed, Mike knew his team had a huge impact, leaving some areas altered for the better.

It was hard to tell how many changes would actually last. Would the US and Pakistani relationship continue to improve? Were the people of the country in a better position to care for themselves in the event of future disasters? In the end, it was clear that out of the rubble of both of the crises Pakistan endured, a chance for a better prepared, more cohesive, and more advanced nation appeared.

Similarly, Concentric evolved rapidly during the pandemic, and some of those changes will become permanent parts of our company. Others will fade away, returning us to older paths or identifying new paths that still lead toward the end game. However, we aren't going back to "normal." We now recognize that the crisis affected our business just as strongly as it affected the world. Things have moved too far to ever go back, and that's okay. The future is still unknown, the path still winding, but we see our goals as clear as ever.

CONCLUSION

THE HARD WORK AHEAD

THE END GAME ISN'T THE FINAL ACT OF THE CRISIS; IT'S where you want to be on the other side.

The end game is the result of your choices and actions and can leave you in a better place than before. It's not easy to think about the end of a crisis when you're still living through one, but you have to keep that strategic goal in mind.

You keep sight of your end game by recognizing where you stand in the crisis timeline. By learning to navigate this predictable—if dynamic—path, you'll have the confidence to make key decisions and lead your team. Knowing each phase of a crisis lets you identify how far along you are and plan your next strategic move.

Most important of all, understand that a crisis ending doesn't mean the challenge is over. It means that the hard work is just beginning.

At the end of this book, we ask you to look back on the lessons you've learned along the way. Think about the new mindset you possess, the confidence you should have in yourself as a leader to navigate any future crisis. We can't predict what is waiting around the next corner, but we can take comfort in knowing that we have prepared.

So where should you begin?

First, you have to know your goals, firmly and clearly. The end game must be a beacon that you can follow in the worst storm. It is a destination that calls to you, even when the world seems to fall apart all around. It is your intent, your guidance that others within your team should understand and affirm. Most of all, it is your north star that will carry you through every twist and turn that may come.

We designed our Edicts for Response as a guide you can follow when you lose your way. By keeping these totems in mind, you can remind yourself and your team that you are not alone. That this disaster, like every other, will one day end.

THE EDICTS FOR RESPONSE
Understand the Anatomy of a Crisis

Remember that every crisis, no matter the scale, follows a pattern. Each phase will require a different mindset and tempo, and the transitions between phases should be monitored carefully lest you backslide.

In the **911 Moment**, be prepared to make quick decisions and tough choices.

In the **Second and Third Order Effects** phase, watch for cascading events that can create new crises all their own.

In the **Steady State**, focus on building toward your end game, gathering intelligence, and positioning yourself for an exit from the crisis.

In the **Reestablishing Normalcy**, ease your transition so you don't overstress your team or yourself. Review the lessons learned, and move forward confidently in an altered world.

Build a Team

Find the right people to fill the positions you will need to succeed. Remember that the role a person fills during normal times might not coincide with their strengths in a crisis. You need to be honest about your own talents, and don't stretch yourself so thin that you can't also be the leader your team needs during this trying time.

Set Communication

Communication is the cornerstone of your crisis management. If you don't consume and disseminate information, you'll be the blind leading the blind. Be specific in your instructions to your team, and create a culture where information is pushed to those that need it and information can easily flow in both directions to you and your team. Reach out to your connections—including competition—to ensure there are strong lines of communication. An unused line can lose its strength, and that can lead to a downfall for both sides.

Intelligence

You need to understand that a crisis means an ever-changing operating picture—not just the situation, but the culture as well. The use of technology and personnel to collect and interpret data is hugely important, no matter what the crisis may be.

Choose your sources wisely, and don't always trust the loudest voices or the ones that tell you what you want to hear. Step outside of your comfort zone and accept that the truth might be difficult to accept. Test your sources to ensure they are accurate, and listen to those on the ground whenever possible. Strong intelligence can give you an edge during the toughest grinds of a crisis.

Refit

Your resources may be limited, and your mission may vary, so you need to be prepared to make do with what you have. Look at your tools, your team, and your business with objective eyes, and be ready to make decisions and take actions that would have seemed outlandish before the crisis. There is a level of confidence and boldness that you need. We are going to try things, and it's okay if they don't work. Make an environment where people are comfortable with experimentation and failure.

Mental Health

These disasters, no matter how small or personal, take a huge toll on all of us. Even if you consider yourself mentally tough, a crisis will chip away until it finally hits a nerve. If you aren't taking care of your mental health, and especially of your team's, you are arming a time bomb. You have to make every effort to care for the people affected by the crisis, especially when most forget to take care of themselves. You have to be ready to deploy support and help your team manage the stress of the crisis mindset.

Relationships

Relationships are a priority at all times and are highlighted even more in stressful or crisis situations. Your relationships will be tested by the chaos, but this is also an opportunity to forge closer bonds and stronger alliances. Make time to connect with your team, your vendors, your clients, and even your rivals. You are all experiencing the same crisis, and you are stronger with greater numbers.

Debt

A crisis requires you to borrow resources you don't have, and they have to be paid back. You also have to understand that debt is not just about material or financial matters. You can create debt in relationships, in mental health, and in goodwill. There are many ways to raise capital in and out of a crisis, and each comes with a list of pros and cons. Research your options so you are able to make informed choices for your future.

The Feedback Loop

Prepare for the event (by reviewing past lessons learned), execute the event, and then review the event for what needs to be sustained or improved and for what happened that you did not expect. Critical review is important for a learning organization.

Be honest and critical—but not personal—of the actions as you recount the good and bad of the past event. Take detailed notes of the choices you made and the consequences of those actions. Most of all, prepare plans and processes that can endure through the next crisis, and test them to ensure they work as proposed.

PRACTICE, PRACTICE, PRACTICE

We've discussed what you need to possess in order to survive and thrive in a crisis, but we haven't addressed one important truth. If you want to gain confidence in these methods, you need to begin practicing them now.

Early in Roderick's career, he had to make high-stress phone calls to raise money for the new business. It's a short conversation with a million-dollar price tag. The pressure is immense, and he struggled. He'd always thought of himself as extroverted, but this was a new skill to master and he simply didn't have the confidence. So he started running drills.

Every day, he would make practice calls. He would ring up a friend or someone in the company and just practice the conversation. Not a script, but attempting to build a genuine connection prior to a transition into business. He'd make small talk, dig a little deeper, and honestly connect to the person at the other end of the line. Then, when it came time to ask for a favor, that social lubricant made it all the easier.

After a few weeks of practice, those high-level calls no longer seemed so impossible. It wasn't that the stakes were any lower, just that he had the individual confidence to push forward. He knew he could handle all aspects of the conversation. And after a few real calls, the process became even easier.

Work with your team and rehearse what you'll do in the next crisis. When that time finally arrives, you'll know what to do and how you want to do it.

PUT THE END GAME FIRST

Concentric was a culmination of all the experiences we had during our lives thus far, and when the current crisis hit, we had plenty of lessons to turn to in creating a proper response. We're no different than you; but we may have had more than our fair share of crises under our belts. Our success came only after we learned from our triumphs and our mistakes. Now you don't have to make the same ones. Take all of this gathered knowledge and use it to plot a path forward rather than retreading where you've already been.

A crisis isn't the end, but rather could be an incredible starting point from which you can define an even clearer path to your end game. You are stronger than the disaster, and you will see the other side. If you take nothing else from this book, remember this:

Every Crisis Will End, and You Choose Where You Stand After

It's almost time to set this book down, so what's next? What are you going to do with this knowledge? Well, we have a few suggestions, if you don't mind.

First, talk to your team. Let them know your intent and your end game. Make sure they understand that the larger goal is a fixed point, but you are flexible on how you arrive. Share these concepts and brainstorm your own crisis plans. What will you do when the world turns upside down? How can you be sure that your company and your people are cared for? How will you know that you will emerge successfully?

Finally, if you found all of this helpful, share the book around. Strength and knowledge aren't meant to be hoarded; they are meant for everyone. Sharing knowledge is power. Build a better, stronger foundation for those around you, and the next crisis won't cause as much fear. When you know what to do and how to proceed, you aren't worried about the chaos. Keep in mind: End Game First!

For more information, and to join us for the continued conversation, come to www.endgamefirst.io.

Email us at info@endgamefirst.io.

SPECIAL THANKS

NO STORY IS TOLD ALONE, AND WE ARE INCREDIBLY grateful for the wonderful people that contributed to make this book possible. We can only hope that we have done justice to their words and experiences.

Jeff Baker, Jim Johnson, Frances Dewing for helping to thoughtfully guide Concentric from the beginning. Laura Hoffner, Monica Palmer, and Lena Gozurian for bringing this book to life.

To all those past and present that helped shape and form our leadership. For those who we worked for, worked with, and had the distinct honor to lead throughout our careers and lives. Without those experiences and events (both goods and... others), we would not have been able to write this book.

ABOUT THE
AUTHORS

MIKE LEFEVER

Vice Admiral (ret.) Mike LeFever, United States Navy, has over forty-five years of public and private sector leadership in high-risk, complex security environments. Mike's success at the intersection of risk, leadership, and technology stems from his experience and expertise in leading disaster relief and humanitarian efforts, the full spectrum of warfare operations, and counterterrorism and counterinsurgency operations. Renowned for building high performance teams, his leadership was directly responsible for numerous significant achievements that protected and enhanced the national security of the United States and private sector growth and profitability.

RODERICK JONES

Roderick began his career with Scotland Yard's Special Branch focused on international terrorism and the close protection of a prominent British cabinet member. Following his move to San Francisco, Roderick founded Concentric and served as CEO for seven years. His work during this period included the design and delivery of comprehensive security programs for a number of high-growth Silicon Valley companies. Roderick serves on the board of advisors for the Center for a New American Security and has a master's degree in Medieval History from Cambridge University.

Printed in the USA
CPSIA information can be obtained
at www.ICGtesting.com
JSHW022002090923
47542JS00006B/9/J